See God Act
The Ministry of Spiritual Direction

Michael Drennan SJ

Published by Messenger Publications, 2021

Copyright © Michael Drennan SJ, 2021

The right of Michael Drennan SJ to be identified as the author of the Work has been asserted by him in accordance with the Copyright and Related Rights Act, 2000.

The material in this publication is protected by copyright law. Except as may be permitted by law, no part of the material may be reproduced (including by storage in a retrieval system) or transmitted in any form or by any means, adapted, rented or lent without the written permission of the copyright owners. Applications for permissions should be addressed to the publisher.

ISBN 9781788124980

Scripture quotations from New Revised Standard Version Bible unless otherwise stated, National Council of the Churches of Christ in the United States of America, used by permission. All rights reserved worldwide.

Designed by Messenger Publications Design Department
Typeset in Garamond Premier Pro
Printed by Hussar Books

Messenger Publications,
37 Leeson Place, Dublin D02 E5V0
www.messenger.ie

Acknowledgements

A special thanks to Messenger Publications, especially Fiona Biggs for her perceptive and helpful suggestions in putting the book into a more coherent format. Thanks also to Carolanne Henry for her work in facilitating the publication.

This book would never have come to birth except for the persistence and encouragement of Mary Hunt, Eileen O'Brien and Aileen Murphy – all co-workers in Manresa. They were like widows with an unjust judge. I thank them for their support and encouragement.

Thanks also to Brendan Comerford SJ, colleague and friend, for his perceptive observations that helped so much to get the thoughts on paper.

I am indebted to my brother Martin for insights and suggestions on some scriptural aspects of the text.

To the many who walked with me over the years, sincere thanks. Your profound questions and enlightened comments continue to develop and clarify my thinking.

There are many unacknowledged sources from lectures heard and books read that have stimulated my thinking over the years. I am grateful to all of you even though I may not remember very well where some ideas originated.

Thanks to the good Lord for the blessings over the years and for giving me the health and will to put these thoughts together. *'Now to him who by the power at work within us is able to accomplish abundantly far more than all we can ask or imagine, to him be glory in the church and in Christ Jesus to all generations, for ever and ever. Amen.'* (Ephesians 3:20–21)

Contents

Introduction 6

1. Journey in Faith 11

2: Relationship with God and Others........................... 26

3: Human Development and Prayer............................. 34

4: Gospel Call to the Human Person 48

5: Discipleship... 57

6: Prayer... 70

7: Spiritual Direction 83

8: Resistance 96

9: Dynamics.. 106

10: Dynamic Patterns in Life..................................... 115

11: Dynamics in Prayer... 125

12: Dynamics in Spiritual Direction 131

13: Dynamics of the Spiritual Director 137

14: The Onward Journey 148

Appendix I: Cases for Discussion 157

Appendix II: The Conversion of Paul 159

Introduction

God, who has given us life, has destined us for the fullness of life (John 10:10). Our lives are interconnected, however, for no one is an island. Our lives affect the lives of others, and our example influences others, just as the example of others has an influence on us. We can be helped by others and be helpful to them.

Support is important in our lives together. Our story is graced by the gift and the presence of the Lord who walks with us. During his time on earth, Jesus interacted with many people, and he has much to say to us who accompany others in faith. He was able to be with the people he met, to accept them where they were, and to lead them onwards from there. Jesus began conversations and interactions with whatever openings were given to him. There are different ways of viewing his interactions and of interpreting experience in the light of these.

As we begin this reflection on the ministry of accompanying others, the journey of the two disciples from Jerusalem to Emmaus (Luke 24:13–35) can provide us with an opening text, as it addresses many aspects of our lives and the place of the Lord in them. As we look to Jesus as our model and guide for walking with others in faith, the Emmaus story tells of a journey that embraced both the human and faith levels. It was an inner as well as an outer journey. Jesus was able to relate to the two disciples and open new horizons for them, leading them to a deeper appreciation of what they had experienced. A new level of meaning emerged that provided them with the energy and incentive for another journey, one that took them back to Jerusalem.

The journey began in an unhappy fashion, with the two despondent disciples commiserating with each other. Then a stranger joined them and asked them what they were talking about. They explained that they had just left Jerusalem, following the ignominy of Jesus' death on the cross and the failure of his mission. Companions in misery, they were now heading for the village of Emmaus, about seven miles from Jerusalem. Central to the Gospel of Luke is the journey Jesus makes *to* Jerusalem (Luke 9:51–18:14). Apart from this journey to Emmaus, there is only one other journey *away from* Jerusalem mentioned in this gospel, the story of the Good Samaritan. It also begins on an unhappy note.

As they left Jerusalem behind, the two disciples had a distorted vision, one that was coloured by their own expectations and hopes, and centred largely on themselves and their own desires. The stranger invited the two of them to share their story and how they interpreted it. They responded readily, relating their version of what had happened, and how their expectations for the redemption of Israel had not been fulfilled, revealing as they did so their misunderstanding of Jesus' mission. They were not convinced by the evidence of the women and their account of a vision of angels and the empty tomb. They were blinded by their own expectations and failed to see beyond them. Their hopes had evaporated, and they were able to do little to help each other.

The stranger responded to their version of events by giving them a very different interpretation of what had happened. He recalled how the prophets had written about a suffering Messiah, and how that was the way to glory. As they listened, something about this stranger and the quality of his interaction was touching their hearts. When they approached the village, however, he left the next move to them. Evening was falling and the disciples sensed that the stranger was ready to go further, so they invited him earnestly to stay with them. He had been good company on the road, and he would be a welcome presence for the evening, providing them with more fruitful conversation. Something was stirring in them, and they were anxious for more. By inviting him to stay, they were expressing their desire.

The revelation took place at table when Jesus took some bread, blessed it, broke it and then gave it to them. They had experienced this before, and it recalled other occasions when they had been present at this gesture. They recognised Jesus, not by his appearance or by his words, but by signs. Then he vanished from their sight. The journey had begun with their failure to recognise Jesus and it ended with their eyes being opened.

The two disciples, by reflecting on their experience, now saw the events that had taken place in a different light. Their hearts were opened, and new life was restored by Jesus' comforting presence, which continued after he had left them. The story did not end there, however. Another desire emerged, and it prompted another journey. They could not wait to get back to Jerusalem, and despite the approach of evening – 'that same hour' – they rushed back to tell the others. Having forsaken the group, they could not wait to get back to tell their story.

This story is a model of discipleship and of Jesus' leadership. Having heard the disciples' human story, including their expectations and their practical interpretation of events, Jesus responded by bringing the conversation to a new level, to the level of faith and the message of the prophets. The story was about more than the two disciples could ever have imagined, because it was an opening to the new. Jesus waited to be invited to stay with them and to share a meal, and it was then that he revealed himself. Jesus moved their hearts, setting them free for the next phase.

All of this helps us have a deeper appreciation of the way the Lord works. Jesus understood the human and practical dimensions of life, but he also knew how to draw on these to lead to a deeper level. Like the disciples, we ask him to walk with us on our journey and to listen to our story, but we also invite him in and allow him to show us the bigger picture. Awareness and reflection add different dimensions to the journey. The Lord broke open the word and later the bread, revealing something of himself through both. His desire for them was revealed through his actions.

This story has much to teach us about accompanying people in the way of the Lord and how we can be a source of strength and comfort to others on their journey. The Lord listened to the two disciples, and then taught and led them to a newer place in faith and life. This is the story of all those who are led by the Lord, but we need awareness and the eyes of faith to appreciate it. Recognising Jesus is central for us and for those we accompany. On our journey with the Lord, desires are important – but they can change, especially when they meet and are transformed by the Lord's own desires.

What follows is a series of reflections on our lives in the Lord. Much of it arises from my experience of working with those who accompany others on the faith journey. As in the Emmaus story, human and practical elements are intertwined with matters of faith and the spiritual. What is presented here draws on insights from Scripture, spirituality and psychology, in order to provide an understanding of the human person in relationship with a loving God, who continues to draw us forward into love and life. God's way is the way of love and freedom, and the invitation is to embrace these in our lives. We live in the Lord and for the Lord, acknowledging that God is present in the whole of life and that the spiritual speaks about life's overall direction. There are human factors that facilitate the loving action of God, just as there are those that impede its reaching its fullness.

There are different options for starting the exploration of spiritual direction. One could begin from a description of the ministry itself, and tease out its implications in the life of a follower of Jesus. There are rich insights available from many sources, past and present, that follow this approach. I propose to start from a somewhat different perspective, however. It will involve exploring first some aspects of the human story, in order to come to a fuller understanding of the human person, while taking account of the faith dimension. It will look to the meeting point of the human story and God's story. It will involve laying foundations – or stepping stones, if you like – that provide a basis for understanding and developing the ministry of spiritual direction. Rather than beginning with spiritual direction, the method employed here means arriving at spiritual direction after the foundations that situate it more fully as a ministry of the faith community have been laid. Then, having looked at spiritual direction itself, the latter part of the book will seek to address some of the dynamics involved in the different relationships – with God, with others and with self.

Spiritual direction and prayer are incarnated in the life of each one of us, and also in the lives of all of us who travel together as a community of faith. It begins from the conviction that God is active in the world and that nothing is impossible to God. The action of God calls for a human response. We need the wisdom to recognise God's surprising ways, the freedom to receive them, and the love to make them a reality through Jesus, who is the way, the truth and the life.

Rather than an academic treatment with footnotes and bibliography, this work is mostly concerned with the practice of spiritual direction. While some chapters will have relevance for any follower of the Lord, the book will apply mostly to those involved in the ministry of spiritual direction.

Michael Drennan SJ
Manresa House
Dublin
July 2021

Chapter 1

Journey in Faith

Life begins in both an individual and communal manner. We come into family settings, localities and countries with different cultural, social and religious dimensions. Our background exercises significant influence on us, especially in the early stages of life, and this has implications for future development. In general, opportunities arise that facilitate our growth into a clearer sense of self, but responses to these opportunities vary for different reasons. Relationships are influential from the beginning and remain important as our story unfolds, but they can change over time and they vary as we go from being dependent to independent to interdependent. The reality of living with others entails being moulded or formed by significant relationships, whether in a positive or negative manner.

Dimensions of the Journey
The direction of one's life can be affected by those who are seen as leaders, those who offer wisdom and direction. Leaders can teach, influence and challenge, as well as guide. Growing in inner freedom is an ideal, and can be realised to some degree, though there are always limits to human freedom. These can come from within or from without, or from both in combination. Nature and nurture are influential in human development, as is the interaction between them. The gifts and qualities we have by birth and from the environment in which we grow can have a constructive or less healthy influence. They can foster growth, they can impede it, or they can lead us to settle for the mediocre.

We can look at life as a journey. While attention can be given to the individual journey, and that is important, we do not travel in isolation. Our lives are intertwined. When we think of a journey, several things come to mind: our travelling companions, the mode of transport, the terrain and the route, as well as the goal of the journey. In the journey of life, there are many factors present that demand our attention, for example our understanding of the human person, the goals or ideals for life that are proclaimed, and the means chosen to attain these goals. There are many other aspects to be taken into account too, such as the private and public dimensions, the individual and communal elements, the internal and external components. Each life is unique, of course, but there are factors that are common to all lives in one way or another, as all of us are human with gifts and limitations.

In looking at any individual life, we can take note of the giftedness that is present, the degree of trust that is evident, the quality of significant relationships, the goals that are operative, the expectations of self and of others, the opportunities and challenges that arise. Sometimes, the external aspects of life – such as success or promotion at work, or living with others – can receive a lot of attention, but the internal aspects, such as growing in freedom, in trust and in peace with oneself, are important too. Dealing with success and failure can involve the internal and the external, and this is true of much of life. The overall harmony or balance in a person's life says a lot about how that person experiences life. Freedom to listen to and learn from experience, as well as the ability to make good decisions, are significant indicators.

If the faith perspective is taken into account, another dimension is added which is interwoven with the human aspects of life. The place of God in a person's life, and the kind of God that is acknowledged, have great significance. It should be noted that, even when God is not explicitly acknowledged, there is a 'god' of some kind present and influential in each life. If it is not the true God, there is another god – whether it be success, power, control or leisure – that exercises its influence and demands time for worship.

Travelling can be adventurous, creative and an opening to something new.

It can remove restrictions, but it can be risky in some conditions. Travel can evoke tension until we have arrived at the desired destination, calling for patience and the willingness to wait. Travelling can be a formative experience, facilitating growth in freedom as we learn more about ourselves, but it can also be a frustrating experience.

Life can be compared to a journey from slavery to freedom. Slavery can have different forms, and external and internal dimensions can be present. Life begins in a self-centred way, and this pattern sometimes continues into adult life. We can remain slaves to our own needs. In that case, we are driven or pushed by factors within to exercise power or control, or to attain satisfaction. There is external slavery, too, such as that caused by a dictatorship or an excessively controlling regime. Such systems of governance allow little room for freedom or individual choice. There can also be a kind of slavery that contains elements of both the external and internal. For example, slavery to work can come from without or from within, or a combination of both.

This description of slavery and of journeying may seem somewhat theoretical, so it may be helpful to look at how some of it was lived out in a real-life situation. In this context, the story of the Israelites in Egypt and their travelling to the Promised Land (as narrated in the books of Exodus, Numbers, Deuteronomy and Joshua) is worthy of reflection. It is presented as the journey of a people from slavery to freedom. Clearly, external slavery was present in the Israelites' exile in Egypt, but there was also internal slavery. Their journey to the Promised Land was both an internal and external journey into freedom.

First Phase in Egypt

As the story began, Egypt, under the new leadership of Pharaoh, was a place of abundance and material prosperity. At an earlier stage, in a time of famine, Egypt had been a place of refuge for the Israelites, and they had enjoyed favour while Joseph's influence prevailed. Over time, however, the situation changed: the Israelites became numerous, and the Egyptians began to fear that they might gain too much control and power. Egypt became a place of fear, oppression and slavery for the Israelites. They were worked hard under strict overseers, and fear of the Egyptians was widespread among them. Power, wealth and control had taken over, and there was little time for God. The Israelites had become slaves, and their desire to worship and offer sacrifices to the Lord seemed to Pharaoh a waste of time, since it would take them away from their work. Hearing the cry of the Israelites, God remembered and was faithful to the covenant made with Abraham: 'Go from your country and your kindred and your father's house to the land that I will show you. I will make of you a great nation, and I will bless you, and make your name great, so that you will be a blessing. I will bless those who bless you, and the one who curses you I will curse; and in you all the families of the earth shall be blessed' (Genesis 12:1–3).

God intervened by calling Moses, who had been rescued from the River Nile as an infant, to lead the people into freedom. Moses did not feel capable of this mission, but the Lord assured him, 'I will be with you' (Exodus 3:12). Later, Moses pleaded with God again, claiming that, since he was a poor speaker, Pharaoh would not listen to him (Exodus 6:30). Time and again, Moses' requests to Pharaoh to set the people free were met with resistance, and Moses needed the Lord's assurance to continue with his task. There ensued a long struggle between the two, with Pharaoh repeatedly refusing permission for Moses' people to leave Egypt. Religious power in Egypt rested with the magicians, whom Pharaoh called upon to respond to the different plagues that befell the people.

There were many challenges for Moses and the people during this first phase of the story in Egypt. Moses was respected by Pharaoh's officials and by his own people (Exodus 11:3), but the interventions of Moses and Aaron through the plagues did little to move Pharaoh's heart. Pharaoh was obstinate because he did not want to lose his workforce. It was not until the Passover, when the firstborn of the Egyptians died, that Pharaoh had a change of heart. The Passover was a major event, and led to the freeing of the Israelites. It would become a feast to be remembered and celebrated each year.

The misery of the Israelites in Egypt was in sharp contrast to the power of Pharaoh. Work had become slavery. The expectation was that the Israelites, having known slavery, would appreciate the freedom the Lord offered them. God allowed them to experience slavery so that they might value freedom. The Israelites faced a great challenge when they arrived at the Red Sea with the Egyptians pursuing them. They complained to Moses for bringing them to this. Moses responded, 'Do not be afraid, stand firm, and see the deliverance that the Lord will accomplish for you today' (Exodus 14:13). They were invited to see what God would do, to see God act. (The title of the book draws on this image.)

Second Phase in the Wilderness

A new phase then began, with the Israelites spending a long time in the wilderness. This was a place of testing for them. They complained about the lack of water, the scarcity of food, the quality of leadership and the unclear direction. They resisted being led by the Lord (Exodus 14:11–12; 16:2–3), and experienced temptations to go back to Egypt, and even to rebel (Numbers 14:9). When new challenges arose, slavery sometimes seemed preferable to them.

The wilderness was a place of transition that found its meaning only in relation to the goal that God desired for the people. In Egypt, they had suffered enslavement – to work, to the Egyptians, to fear and to failure. Now, having been set free from that slavery, they were being set free from non-essentials. The desert was a time of purification where they were being set free to worship God in freedom. The journey was one of adventure, of discovery and of pilgrimage, for God was with them. It was a journey into poverty, where they would meet God in a new way, as Saviour. It had a goal, since they were the chosen people heading to a new land (Exodus 6:7–8). The goal of the journey was not just the land, however, but God (Exodus 19:4). The journey involved a deeper liberation. It meant taking a risk, involving the loss of security, but it opened the way to something greater.

The struggle and resistance of the Israelites was evident throughout the journey, even prompting them to make and worship a golden calf. God's fidelity and support remained constant, however. God was providing for them, and continued to communicate with them through Moses. God was present to them in a pillar of cloud and a pillar of fire, guiding them day and night. God's support was made manifest in various ways:

- The water that God provided for them as a gift (Exodus 15:17).
- The manna which, as food for the journey, was a sign of God's care for them (Exodus 16).
- The ark, which was a promise of God's presence among them (Exodus 40).
- The Covenant, which was a promise of God's protection. (The Covenant gave the people an identity and implied shared values. Seeking security in God, they were God's people.)
- The Ten Commandments, which gave direction to Israel's response to God. (The basic Commandment was to love and trust God alone.)

The Israelites were challenged by having to face a new situation as they left Egypt and spent a long time in the wilderness. There was the tension of the journey itself, since the Promised Land was not attained as quickly as they would have liked. God was actively present with them, however. The people were led and carried. In the absence of any external signposts, God was the signpost indicating the way. The journey had a goal, but the final goal was more than the land; the final goal was God: 'You have seen what I did to the Egyptians, and how I bore you on eagles' wings and brought you to myself. Now therefore, if you obey my voice and keep my covenant, you shall be my treasured possession out of all the peoples. Indeed, the whole earth is mine, but you shall be for me a priestly kingdom and a holy nation' (Exodus 19:4–6). The entry into the new land confirmed God's choice of the Israelites. The delays on the way were caused by their lack of faith.

God provided what was needed for the Israelites, but they had to wait on God to be able to enter the new land, for it was God's gift to them. On the way, their expectations were challenged and, at times, they were tempted to go back. However, the call was to march on, although they did go around in circles at times (Deuteronomy 2 and 3). Despite their resistance, God's way prevailed in the end.

In the midst of many struggles, the people retained hope in Moses as their leader. Moses was a prophetic leader who taught, reassured, challenged and energised the people, a liberator who kept the vision of God to the fore. A spiritual and social leader, he had a significant role in the lives of the Israelites, as mediator between God and the people and between the people and God. His relationship with God was central to the mission he had received. Moses could intercede with God and pray in solidarity with his own people, even when they themselves had failed, as happened when they relapsed into idolatry (Exodus 32). Moses was able to interpret events for the people. He challenged them when they resisted, even though, at one point, they were almost ready to stone him (Exodus 17:4).

The Third Phase in the Promised Land
Their arrival in the new land under Joshua, Moses' successor, heralded a new beginning for the people. In one sense the journey had ended, but it did not really end then, since the people were to live out their lives from now on as a covenant people whom God had rescued from slavery. On coming into the Promised Land an important new element emerged for them: the need to remember what God had done for them and to reflect on the journey. They were not just to repeat their story, but to learn from it. The people renewed their decision to serve God, and they affirmed their commitment to one another (Joshua 24:14–24). Ratifying choices made earlier helped them keep the commitment alive.

The chosen people were invited to recall how 'in the wilderness, the Lord your God carried you, just as one carries a child, all the way you travelled until you reached this place' (Deuteronomy 1:31). The Book of Deuteronomy many times counsels the people to remember and not to forget: 'Remember the long way that the Lord your God has led you these forty years in the wilderness' (8:2). The temptation of their new prosperity was to forget, but this journey was too important to be forgotten. Recognising God's goodness to them would help them live in a spirit of gratitude in God's land. This land was not theirs; it was God's gift. Having known external slavery, it was presumed they would value freedom. They were to express their gratitude by caring for the most vulnerable among them: the widow, the orphan and the stranger.

The people's journey did not end with the crossing of the Jordan and their arrival in the Promised Land (Joshua 3). Their entry into the Promised Land confirmed God's choice of Israel, reminding them that God was faithful to the promises made to them. They were urged to use this land, which was God's gift to the whole community, well. It was to be a place of rest where work would no longer be a burden (Deuteronomy 5:15; 11:10–11). The land became a temptation, however, because the people tended to forget that it was a gift. Afraid of the demands made, they began to grasp and exploit it, seeking to eliminate the mystery by worshipping false gods. The call was to fidelity and justice, but the temptation was to forget once they had arrived. The land was a gift, but it could be lost, as would happen later at the time of exile. Even worse, by choosing to go their own way and by following false gods, the people could lose the inner gift of being God's covenant people. By losing their freedom, a new form of slavery could take over.

A Reflection on Their Journey

The Exodus journey was made in stages, with particular milestones or crossing points. Some of these milestones were more evident externally. The Passover was one key moment that was to be remembered and celebrated. Other major moments were crossing the Red Sea as they escaped from Egypt, and crossing the River Jordan to enter the Promised Land. In between, there were times when the people were challenged by Moses to let God lead and guide them. When their own interests dominated, rebellion in various forms manifested itself in their responses. Situations of transition heightened their anxiety, and they became more concerned about themselves. There was an unwillingness on their part to wait, or to go at God's pace. Waiting was seen as a waste of time, rather than something formative in preparing for a fuller reception of the gift on offer. Sometimes the people wanted to go back, and at other times they wanted to push forward prematurely. Eager to complete the journey in their own way, the delay in arriving proved a great challenge to them.

The people and Moses were changed through that journey, and their relationships were different as a result. The message that God was present on their journey was clear. God took the initiative and was committed to them. God made a covenant with them, giving them an identity as a people, so that a bond was formed with God and with each other. The covenant was broken and renewed many times, but God remained faithful to them. Their infidelities and failures were more evident than their successes on that journey, but God's way prevailed and they did enter the land promised to them. What was clear was the desire of God to lead the people to freedom and to a new relationship. Now work was to be service, rather than the slavery it had been in Egypt. They were to live and work in a new way, choosing to serve God through it.

The Exodus journey speaks to any group of people, since there are elements in it that are common to any human story. It is a helpful background to understanding the Church as the People of God, for example, with its emphasis on the communal dimension of the Church. The Exodus journey was an internal as well as an external one, since the slavery the people experienced was internal as well as external. The external aspect of slavery in Egypt was obvious, but internal slavery became more evident as the journey progressed, when the people wanted their own way and complained about what was not to their satisfaction. They were called to be dependent on God, to find security in God, and not in themselves. The Passover had a meaning beyond the immediate event of their liberation by Pharaoh. It was a feast that challenged oppressive relationships and idolatry of all kinds.

Slavery can take different forms in the human story. There can be slavery to others, to burdensome work, to fear, to our own opinion, to our own expectations, to wanting our own way. The desire to be in control that is so prominent in the human story can be another form of slavery. The chosen people in the wilderness thought they knew better, objecting to the direction in which they were taken, the food they were given and the quality of their leadership. There was murmuring and complaining as they lamented the 'good old days' in Egypt. It became a great challenge for them to travel at God's pace, in God's direction, in dependence on God. As they journeyed into the unknown, the wilderness was a place of testing, and a time of transition. They would have to empty themselves if they were to have space for God, and that did not come easily to them. Internal space became more challenging than external space. The words of Dag Hammarskjöld are appropriate: 'The longest journey is the journey inwards.'

The Exodus story reminds us that in life there are gifts and challenges from within and from without, and that many factors come into play. There are stages in our lives as there were for the Israelites on their journey from Egypt to the Promised Land.

- The first stage, getting out of Egypt, was focused on being set free from the external slavery of work and oppression. The Passover and the crossing of the Red Sea were profound moments of transition through God's intervention.
- The next phase was the long time in the wilderness, with its many challenges. There was a struggle to accept God's direction and to move at God's pace on the journey. Becoming dependent on God and living as a people of the Covenant did not come easily to them. An agreement was made, but they soon broke it as they resisted God's way.
- Arrival in the Promised Land presented them with a new situation. It was God's land and a gift shared with them but, as they tended to think of it as their own land, it presented them with an ongoing struggle. The call to remember, to reflect and to be grateful was frequently put before them. They were to show their gratitude by caring for the most vulnerable among them.

There is an underlying pattern throughout the various stages. In both the external and internal struggles the people wanted to be in control and to be able to decide for themselves. This found expression in each of the stages. Different situations manifested the same underlying pattern, with a common thread running through them. Each new stage or situation provided an opportunity and a challenge. Moving on interiorly was much more difficult than going ahead externally. The desire to be in control did not die easily.

Our Journey

The journey of the Israelites, with their gifts and struggles, continues to be relevant in our time. Life involves being and becoming, stability and change, time to rest and time to move on, times of crisis and times of celebration. There is always some element of transition present, as external situations change and changes take place within us when negotiating those transitions. In dealing with such situations, we can respond well or poorly; we can progress or regress. It is futile to try to stay still, just as it is difficult to remain still when swimming against a strong current in a river. While there is some stability in life, much of our time is lived in transition, and a great deal depends on the quality of the decisions we make in times of change.

The Exodus journey is revealing for all of us. We are on a journey as a people. From a faith perspective, as well as from the state of the environment, we can see the world around us as a wilderness. The presence of false gods is evident. For many, worship is a waste of time. People are enslaved to work in different ways. Fear is dominant for many. Security, which is meant to be found in God, is sought more readily in what is ephemeral. We are tempted to place our trust in all sorts of things, especially when we experience the wilderness. For example, there are people who, finding themselves unhappy with leadership in the world and in the Church, bemoan the passing of the 'good old days'. They forget and complain.

In the ups and downs of our lives, in our failures and hopes, there is need for a deeper faith in the God who continues to be faithful to us. Since we have not yet arrived, we can resist transition, and tension is present as we journey. We can become frustrated and find it difficult to cope. We can try to carry too much from the past. In our vulnerability, our trust and commitment are tested. The challenge is to move at God's pace, and to learn to rely more fully on God, finding our true identity in the New Covenant, ratified by Jesus. Being given more freedom does not mean that we know how to use it well. We can stay in the wilderness, failing to see God present in it. New forms of slavery can entrap us.

It is important to look on our journey, with all its stages, through the eyes of faith, and see how God is in it. This is often clearer in retrospect. In our lives, there are key moments, significant people, milestones and turning points that manifest more clearly God's guidance on our journey from slavery to freedom. While there are *external* factors in our enslavement – how we are restricted by others – much of our lack of freedom is *internal*. We can be held bound by many elements within ourselves, such as fear, anxiety or insecurity. It is of great importance that we, and those we accompany, grow in inner freedom, for it facilitates the outer dimension in the transitions of life; it helps us recognise the gift of God who is faithful. Reflecting on our own story serves to deepen our faith and to appreciate the loving action of God in our lives and in the lives of others. Taking time and space for this reflection helps to clarify our focus for the ministry of spiritual direction, and it makes us better companions on the journey.

Moments of light and darkness, success and failure, planned events and surprises – these have all made up part of our story. They form a tapestry that has its own beauty, but it also has limitations. Like all tapestries, loose threads are more visible from the reverse side. We can see things better in hindsight, as happened for Jacob after his dream (Genesis 28:17), or the two disciples when they recognised Jesus at Emmaus (Luke 24:31). Desiring to grow in appreciation of where God has been in the story, we pause to look back. Reflection enables us to see more clearly, or differently.

Different events move us to take on a new direction, a new venture. Some of these ventures may be challenging or difficult. Success may not encourage creative thinking, while failure can become the springboard of change. Times of crisis can inspire generosity and bring out the best in people. Like the Israelites, who were reminded of all God had done for them, we too are to remember and be grateful, expressing this by caring for the most vulnerable among us. We are reminded to be generous in living our covenant relationship with God. Desire is important for us, as it indicates that we want something different or new. It can also open us to God's transforming desire for us.

As we reflect, we need to remember that, as was true for the Israelites, God is in the wilderness today. Isaiah spoke of the desert being in bloom when he wrote of the return of the exiles from Babylon (Isaiah 35). The wilderness is a place of testing, but it is also the place in which to find God. It can deepen our sense of reality and help us to find a clearer perspective, stripping away false securities and highlighting the essentials. The wilderness reveals a great deal to us – of ourselves, of God and of our world – as well as challenging what is selfish and passing. The inward journey can be nourished in the wilderness, as suggested in the words of Hosea: 'I will now allure her, and bring her into the wilderness, and speak tenderly to her' (Hosea 2:14).

The wilderness is a place of revelation and of mission. New missions began there. With his proclamation of repentance, John the Baptist started his ministry in the wilderness, where he lived simply by eating what the place provided, locusts and wild honey. Jesus' mission began in the wilderness, with his baptism by John. Jesus' temptations took place in the wilderness, where he showed in his response the kind of Messiah he would be. The wilderness was a place in which things happened. It was not a place of escape, but a school of learning and of formation for mission.

Our journey through the wilderness is one of discovery of God, of ourselves and of each other, so that we may be good companions on the way. It invites us to discover and unwrap the gift, so that we might appreciate the journey more fully. That inner journey invites us to look at our images of God and ourselves, and to clarify our call. Our relationships and our prayer are important realities, both in our lives and in our ministry of service to others in Jesus' name.

Life is an ongoing journey for us, and going out is basic to the human experience. It involves leaving the familiar behind and embarking on something new. For the Israelites Egypt was not a homeland. God was calling them to move elsewhere. The Exodus was a saving event led by God, who called and guided the people in love. It was God who took the initiative, and that applies to us and to our mission at this time. We can profit from reflection on the Exodus story, learning about God's initiative, the human response, the role of leadership and guidance, and how to be a people of the

Covenant supporting one another on the journey. We have our phases of life, our transitions and our Passover in Jesus, but we also have the ability to forget, to lose direction. Loss of faith led to loss of direction for the Israelites, and that can happen to us too. The capacity to lose the gift remains, to drift back into another form of slavery, but that is not the Lord's desire for us.

We are called to live the giftedness given to us, to listen, to let God's word shape our lives and our identities. The story of Exodus provides a good example, speaking as it does about the individual and communal journey of life, and how to deal with the internal as well as the external slavery that we find. Living out our gifts and struggles in a faith context, the overall framework of life reveals to us a faithful God, who is bonded with us in a covenant relationship. We struggle, and many times we fail to keep our side of the agreement. Nevertheless, God remains faithful. Exodus calls us to come home to God and to ourselves in the new land that God has prepared for us.

The story of Exodus teaches us much about God, about our relationship with God and with one another, as well as the dynamics involved in these relationships. The gift of God can be welcomed, but it can be lost, too, when we choose to go our own way. The story provides a good foundation for self-understanding, for understanding others, and for fostering growth in the way of the Lord. We travel together, desiring to be good companions to those we accompany on the journey of life to the land the Lord has promised to us.

Reflection

What are the milestones of my journey?
Where am I on the journey inwards?

Chapter 2

Relationship with God and Others

Reflection on the journey of life invites us to appreciate our gifts as well as our areas of struggle, so that we can grow in openness to the Lord and to his way. During their time in the wilderness, the chosen people were changed in their relationship with God, with Moses and with each other. Sometimes these changes were positive but, on other occasions, that was not so. The Commandments taught them about a God of love who called them into a true relationship with God and with each other. They reminded them that God was close to them, was concerned about them and was committed to them. Their image of God underwent change, as did their relationship with God. The covenant made them into a people bonded with the Lord in a special way. The law of love was to guide their relationships. While that did guide them at times, on other occasions they went their own way, even making and worshipping false gods. Selfish interests took precedence at times, and the bigger vision was lost. All of this is evident in the Exodus story.

Similarly, we are made in the image of God with the potential to grow. As people of the New Covenant we are given a special dignity, and invited to a closer relationship with God. Our image of God and of the self can undergo change. Growing in self-knowledge, we can expand the freedom we have to respond to the Lord in living the commandment of love. We can also go our own way, however, by finding and worshipping false gods. The choices we make and the direction we take have implications for our relationships with the Lord and with each other. By reflecting on our experience and learning from it, the way is opened to change and more faithful living in the truth the Lord reveals to us.

A desire is present in all of us to live in right relationships with ourselves, with God, with others and with all of God's creation. This means we desire to live justly, although living out this basic human desire challenges us and invites us to change. These relationships – with God, self and others – are part of a dynamic process that gives momentum and direction to our lives. Unless there are blocks or impediments that prevent change and growth, they are not static. It could be said that a relationship that is too stable is a dead relationship, as too much stability gets in the way of growth and change.

Life involves movement and growth. As life brings up new situations and new relationships, we have the facility to see and respond in new ways. There is a movement within ourselves that leads us onwards, as well as external stimuli that invite further growth. Life involves 'becoming' as well as 'being', change as well as stability, the new as well as the old. Life is not mere repetition, and to live is to change. Just as we grow physically, we are meant to grow in many other ways as well: intellectually, emotionally and in inner freedom. Growth in these areas is more challenging than physical growth, since it does not occur automatically. It opens up the deeper areas of life, where change has implications for the quality of our relationships.

We can learn from the pattern of human relationships. If a relationship is to continue in a life-giving way, a change in one person requires a change in the other. Change can be initiated by some new insight, a different situation, or the presence of a crisis; it can also come gradually over time, so that the awareness of it only becomes evident later on. We can accept change in another, or we can try to impede this change, wanting the other to remain as of old. When there is an adjustment in a relationship, there is a change in the manner of *communication* between those involved. When the bond is strengthened, there will be a deeper level of communication and a growth in respect; when the connecting points are weakened, the opposite occurs.

Consider a concrete situation. If I come to see myself or the other person differently, this will affect our relationship, and bring about a change of one kind or another in how we interact. If I am unsure of myself or feel under threat, that will manifest itself in my attitudes, words and actions, whereas if I am comfortable in myself that will manifest itself too. I can allow the other person the freedom to be different, or I can try to keep the relationship as it was. Either response will influence the quantity of freedom in the relationship, as well as the level of communication. Movement can be facilitated or impeded. A reflective way of living can facilitate change in the self, and help bring about change in the relationship with others and with the Lord.

Image of Self and of God
It is important to see how we experience ourselves and to note any change that has occurred in our perception. The words of Paul illustrate the change that is expected to occur: 'When I was a child, I spoke like a child, I thought like a child, I reasoned like a child; when I became an adult, I put an end to childish ways' (1 Corinthians 13:11). During the course of my development from childhood into adulthood, it is important to remember that there is continuity in my sense of myself, as well as openness to change and growth. There is both 'being' and 'becoming'. However, growth is not automatic, since it can be blocked or impeded to varying degrees. Everybody struggles with their sense of self and with accepting the limitations of being a creature, but fears and doubts do not necessarily block all movement. Transitions are to be negotiated.

In human life, our sense of self can be quite fragile, since it touches the many areas that highlight our need to accept limits, incompleteness and vulnerability. Our sense of self can be influenced by many factors, including background, work, position, promotion, achievement, friendships and being needed (or not). Coming to a healthy sense of self is an ongoing process. Becoming more at home with ourselves, so that we can live in peace with our own limitations and with those of others, helps foster openness and trust in the journey of life. Trust in self and trust in others are linked in some way, as is trust in God. Coming to a true appreciation of ourselves as created by God in love and for love is an ongoing venture. In the process, it is good to remember that, being created in the image of God who is mystery, we never fully understand ourselves or each other. There is always a mysterious dimension to our own lives and the lives of others.

Our sense of God can change also, as can our sense of others. At Caesarea Philippi, Jesus invited Peter to give a personal response when he asked him, 'Who do you say I am?' Peter's reply was a wonderful expression of faith: 'You are the Messiah, the Son of the living God' (Matthew 16:15-16). Nevertheless, this answer would develop for Peter as he pondered its implications after he had experienced the passion, death and resurrection of Jesus. At the Lord's invitation, a deeper level of meaning would emerge. The Lord's relationship with Peter was not static, just as God is not static in relationship with us. God is continually inviting us, sharing love with us, taking the initiative in calling us, desiring the best for us. The Lord knows our potential and calls us beyond a childhood image.

Our early sense of God tends to come from outside ourselves, from our parents, teachers and other significant people in childhood. An early impression is formed, not only from what these adults say explicitly about God, but also from how they are: loving, close and understanding, or demanding, challenging and distant. Our sense of God can be coloured by all of that. Some image is being portrayed through it all, and is being formed and becoming operative in us. God may be portrayed as close or distant, as demanding or forgiving, as one to fear or as one who loves. As we grow, new influences emerge and more information is gathered, but it takes time to formulate our own image of God. Even then, the process is ongoing, because we continue to be drawn into the mystery of God. Growth in freedom is part of life and, as we grow, our image of God changes, as does the quality of our relationship with God. In that way, what may have been an impression of a God of fear can become, over time, one of a God of love.

Relationship with God
We live in relationships – with God, self, others and all that God has made – but these relationships can change over time. Communication of depth and

quality is important in bringing relationships to a deeper level. A growing sense of self and of God is important for our quality of life and for our direction in life. Growth enables us to ask at a deeper level, 'How do I want to live in relationship with God and others?' This question focuses our life-direction, our fundamental option, and it leads to a choice that will guide our other choices, which, in turn, will facilitate us in living out that basic decision. For example, the decision to get married will lead to many more decisions as that commitment is lived out.

Our image of ourselves is always in relation to the image of God and of others, either directly or inversely. A poor sense of self can be related to a demanding God who cannot be pleased. A scrupulous person, for example, has a twice-exaggerated image – a negative image of self, and an image of a God who cannot be satisfied. In that situation, the gap between God and the self is too wide, and is a constant source of frustration. Others can have an inflated sense of self, with the concomitant image of a God who is comforting, but not challenging. As a result, very little changes in these people. Most people fit somewhere between those two extremes, moving forward slowly, generally in fits and starts.

Sometimes our images of self and God can be different in different situations, or in response to different events. We tend to have predominant images of self and God, but these can change somewhat when something significant happens, such as a crisis. This sometimes leads to the images becoming more rigid or defensive, but at other times it can loosen up these images, when the focus is taken off the self out of concern for the plight of others. The change may be short-lived, however, like a building that stabilises again following the shock of an earthquake.

The reality of life is that we all struggle in some way, whether to accept love, to believe that we are lovable, or to get beyond fears of some kind, whether of failure or of rejection or of love itself. The freedom to recognise these and to lessen their influence is the desired way forward. For this to happen it may be necessary to uncover blocks that often have their roots in childhood experiences, and in that case the help of another person may be necessary in order to bring these blocks more fully into awareness.

Relationships need time and good communication to develop. It means allowing the self and the other to change, so that a different quality of presence and of communication can emerge. As they go deeper, relationships may move from the use of many words to the need for few words. The same is true of our relationship with God, as God becomes more real and is experienced as closer.

Prayer

Our relationship with God involves our whole life, but it finds a particular expression in prayer. As changes take place in how we experience ourselves, there will be adjustments in how we relate to God too. An experience of God's love can lead to a changed relationship with God and, in turn, a change in our prayer and our sense of self. Was Moses the same after the vision of the burning bush (Exodus 3:1–6), or were Peter, James and John no different following Jesus' transfiguration (Matthew 17:1–8)? It is clear that Saul was not the same following his experience on the road to Damascus (Acts 9:1–9). He was drawn beyond his comfort zone to a new way of relating and living. Change for Saul came quickly, but it often comes about gradually, over time. It is helpful for each of us to reflect on the changes that have occurred over the years, and to note significant times or events that were influential on the journey.

If our image of ourselves changes, then our image of God will change, too, as will our prayer; and we will relate differently to others as well. All these elements are interconnected and influence each other. Noticing what is happening in us facilitates movement in response to the action of the Lord. Prayer that is 'real' and linked with life will help open the doors to change, or will help us to notice what gets in its way. It will take the main focus off ourselves and how we *have to be*, or how we *should be* in prayer and in life. Time is necessary if we are to break the notion that some day 'I will get it right'. We continue to acknowledge our need of God, so that we can let God lead.

When prayer is linked with life it leads to change in other areas, such as our sense of self and of God. If we are more trusting, we pray differently than if fear predominates, so that trust can grow and fear can decrease. The form and quality of communication can change over time. The language of a child is not that of an adult, and the response of an adult should be different in many ways from that of a child. Saying prayers is not the same as praying. Over time, God's desires can become more central in our prayer, with a diminishing focus on the self. Bringing the real issues of life to prayer involves an opening to change in all the relationships considered here – with self, God and others.

The parable of the Pharisee and the tax collector (Luke 18:9–14) is a helpful text in considering how prayer is related to our image of self and our image of God, and indeed how these elements are all connected. It is worth quoting the whole parable here:

'Two men went up to the temple to pray, one a Pharisee and the other a tax collector. The Pharisee, standing by himself, was praying thus, "God, I thank you that I am not like other people: thieves, rogues, adulterers, or even like this tax collector. I fast twice a week; I give a tenth of all my income." But the tax collector, standing far off, would not even look up to heaven, but was beating his breast and saying, "God, be merciful to me, a sinner!"'

Here we see how different perceptions of self and of God lead to diverse ways of prayer. The Pharisee sees himself as good, just and faithful to the Commandments, unlike the tax collector. His prayer is focused on himself, rejoicing in his own goodness and giving thanks for it. He is the focus of his own prayer, and God is made in the Pharisee's own image and likeness. In contrast, the tax collector in his prayer acknowledges his own situation as a sinner. He recognises God as God, and asks for mercy. Acknowledging his need, his disposition is humble, honest and open to the gift of God. A real meeting takes place between the tax collector and God. The tax collector comes as he is, accepting his true situation and his need of God's mercy.

Growth in the sense of self and sense of God will have implications for other relationships too. Being more comfortable in one's own skin and accepting the limitations of life can lead to greater respect in all relationships, acknowledging the gifts of others, and living in greater harmony with them. In the parable above, the Pharisee, by comparing himself to the tax collector, is being judgemental and competitive rather than cooperative. With God as his focus, the tax collector makes no reference to the Pharisee in his prayer. This suggests that he has less need than the Pharisee to be in control, and less reason to exploit. He has a better appreciation of all that is given to him. That is the attitude that Jesus praises and offers as an example.

This approach enables more freedom and a clearer set of values to be brought to bear on our lives and on our decisions. It makes it easier for us to deal with the changing nature of life in a healthier way. Growth in the understanding of self, of others and of God is part of the journey, and reflection and review will bring more clarity as we look back on our faith journey. By noting change in how we experience God, or in our sense of self as made in God's image, or in prayer itself, we are invited to make the link between them. This opens up the wider dimension of these relationships and the richness contained in them. The link between prayer and life becomes more obvious.

Reflection

How has my prayer changed?
How do I see myself and God now?

Chapter 3

Human Development and Prayer

We have looked at the relationship between self and God, and how prayer is central to this relationship on our faith journey. Now it will be helpful to come to an understanding of the person who prays and what influences may be active in our relationships with God and with others. As the parable of the sower illustrates (Matthew 13:4–9), people have different responses to the word of God, reflected in a range of images, from rocky place to fertile ground with a bountiful harvest. Within ourselves, however, different aspects of these responses can be present, as we can have more freedom in some areas of life than in others. Each of us is gifted, but we each also have some area, or areas, where we are more liable to be less responsive. For example, being too busy in life can lead to loss of direction and less fruitfulness. In other words, there are different levels of freedom in each person in response to the gifts God offers. The degree of freedom influences the response evoked.

While there are some elements common to all of our lives, we know that each person has individual characteristics too, and a unique story. As human beings, we are gifted, though limited, creatures. Our particular characteristics, our backgrounds and how we were nurtured and formed exert their influence on us. Our formation in faith has an important role in providing direction and in setting goals in life. There are challenges to all of this from various sources, inside and outside ourselves. It is good to remember that in his ministry Jesus met, not only openness and receptivity, but also blindness and resistance. The response to his call was not always immediate and generous.

We can speak of a desire for wholeness and holiness in life, although these are not the same. Nearness to God cannot be equated with psychological health. Nevertheless, psychology has something to offer in helping us to understand human life with its vision, its ideals, its limits and its ambiguities, and also how we relate to others. Psychology helps us to appreciate the freedom we need in order to receive and respond to the word of God and to grow in it. In general, people are not totally free or totally unfree, but somewhere in between. It is possible for us to change, however, so that the area of freedom can either be enlarged or further restricted. The Johari Window (below) illustrates areas of freedom in life, while also suggesting others that are restricted. It highlights aspects of life that are open (public), hidden (private), blind and unconscious. All four areas are present in each person.

The Johari Window

	KNOWN TO SELF	UNKNOWN TO SELF
KNOWN TO OTHERS	OPEN (Public knowledge; what I show you)	BLIND (Feedback; your gift to me)
UNKNOWN TO OTHERS	HIDDEN (Private; mine to share if I trust you)	UNCONSCIOUS (Unknown; new awareness can emerge)

The diagram gives some insight into the human person, and provides a framework for further discussion when we look at what may influence a person's prayer.

Psychology and sociology have contributed to our understanding of human development. In looking at formulated theories, however, it has to be stated that most of them are humanistic, in the sense that they do not set out to include God or the spiritual aspect in their theories. The end goal for them, and for psychology in general, is human maturity or freedom in some form or other. The many theories that are proposed vary in the degree of freedom they allow and the capacity for change they see as possible. At one extreme, there are approaches that are pessimistic in tone, seeing the person as having little freedom and being 'driven' by needs. Other approaches are more positive, acknowledging the presence of a capacity for change if the right conditions are present. All approaches have something to offer, but our starting point here is the claim that human freedom is *freedom within limits*. Growth in maturity can be inferred from a person's ability to take responsibility and to respond to situations rather than reacting to them, and also by the quality of relationships with authority figures and with others.

When the human person is seen in a Christian context, a further dimension is added, since God is now perceived as the end goal, rather than ourselves. Giving glory to God, or serving Christ, is different from finding ourselves or fulfilling ourselves, though the two can be related. In the Christian perspective, one is the means to the other – it is in losing ourselves that we find ourselves (John 12:25). Before we can lose it, however, we have to have some sense of the self. Since theories of psychology and human development facilitate the emergence of an identity, it may be of some help at this point to take a brief look at what they have to offer, as aids to coming to know and understand ourselves better. Then we will look at how this can be related to growth in the Lord, and to an identity that is related to him and that finds its meaning in him.

Process of Development
Life begins in a dependent manner. A child needs love, food, care and security from another or others. This is crucial for growth and the development of trust and a sense of worth. There are basic needs or tendencies that are

part of being human – they encompass the biological (hunger and thirst, for example) and the sociological (the need for relationship with others). If these needs are not met, fear, insecurity, dependency or a defensive kind of independence can prevail. Particularly dominant in the earlier years are emotional factors, such as likes and dislikes, with the immediate needs to the fore. Initially, the child demands instant gratification, and that is usually granted. As time goes on, however, this gratification tends to be delayed. This is part of a formative process, although the child may not readily accept it. A socialisation process is taking place, through which the child learns to relate in a way that takes others into account. The world is no longer simply a place for 'me', 'mine' and 'my own' immediate gratification.

Experience begins with life. It is present from the beginning, so a great deal has gone on in the child at the emotional level before the development of reason, which is understood to come around the age of eight. This means that patterns are laid down early in the family about what matters, who is important, and how to relate. A child picks up what can or cannot be talked about, what can be said at home but not elsewhere, what can be done or not done in the presence of parents. Attitudes and values are picked up about how to relate, who or what is important and who is to be trusted. Good habits are learned as well as less good ones. A child 'learns' a way of dealing with life, whether it is a good way or not. In fact, it is generally a mixture of the good and the defensive.

Initially, the child is quite open about what to say but, in time, this tends to change, depending to some extent on the 'training' given and the quality of relationships experienced. When trust is present a healthier sense of self develops, and more adaptive ways of dealing with life will exist. On the other hand, if trust is weak, less adaptive – or even maladaptive – ways of coping with what life brings up may develop. Everyone seeks a sense of worth, but how it is sought has great significance. Images of God and self, as well as how to relate to others, are coloured by early experience.

Less accepted patterns can be protected by *defences* that screen them off – for example, by lying about having done something, or blaming another for it. The inability to take responsibility can become a pattern, while the reason for doing something can either be outside of our awareness (unconscious) or barely within our awareness. It then becomes an 'automatic' reaction rather than a clear choice. Other early patterns can remain evident in adulthood, such as an excessive need to achieve, unease with anger, fear of not being successful, or the need to lead. For some people, fear can become too influential in dealing with a situation. These patterns become more evident when they are encountered in an exaggerated way.

All of this means that the failure to be truthful and to take responsibility is not limited to children, nor is the inability to delay gratification. Influences from childhood can continue in a new form, meaning that human life is complex, and much ambiguity is evident in it. For example, an absence of love in childhood can lead to the same result as being 'smothered in love': a lack of belief in self, and an over-reliance on others for one's self-worth. Needing to be loved and to be needed at all costs leaves a person very dependent.

Life continues to present new situations, new opportunities and new relationships that can continue the growth process, but these may be blocked by fears, doubts or anxiety. The ability to deal with change, while availing of adequate support, is part of the growth process. As a child moves from one stage of life to another – from home to school, for example – a new challenge is presented. School seeks to move a child forward gradually; the task is never too far ahead, but is proportionate to the child's present situation. A child who is unable to deal with what is new may regress to a previous way of handling such situations, for example crying or sulking.

Growing up is more than a physical phenomenon, but chronological age and mental age are not necessarily the same. Childish behaviour can be observed in adults. The level of development and the degree of freedom (that are present) are indicated by how we see ourselves, how we relate to others, and the image of God that is present. There is usually some relationship between self-image and the image of God, though the relationship here can vary. Both images may be very idealistic; or a poor sense of self may be found with a demanding God ('I should be perfect … I shouldn't feel this'); or an inflated sense of self can go hand in hand with a 'comfortable' God.

Emotion is significant and important in life, but we also have the capacity to reason. We can think, we can abstract and we can be moved by ideas. The emotional and rational are both part of us; they can influence each other, can be manifested in the body and can lead to action. For example, anger can lead to unclear thinking, can be physically evident in a flushed face, and can lead to action. Thinking can also influence feeling. Either can dominate. Feeling, thinking and bodily manifestation can be going on at the same time, and it is helpful to note that they are interconnected in a dynamic relationship, since they influence each other and can lead to external expression. Each one – thinking, feeling, the body and behaviour – can reveal something of what is happening. Taking note of this can help us to understand what is going on in a particular situation.

What is going on may not be clear-cut, however, because one element can be screened off from another, especially the emotional from the rational, and its influence not noted. For example, good reasons may be given for doing something or avoiding it – be it feasting or fasting, taking action or not – but emotion may be the real influence at work. Emotion can prevail over reason, when the immediate attraction prevails over what is believed to be good in the long term; the opposite can also occur where the appeal of the immediate is noted but the choice is made to forego it. The latter is more difficult when the affective component is very strong or not noticed; for example, we can be driven by the need to succeed, without being aware of it; in that case, we may find ourselves staying up half the night to complete something that is objectively of no great importance, but may be significant symbolically. When we are aware of the emotional push, we can go against it. We might wish to finish a particular project, but by accepting that we do not have the time to complete it as we would like, we may settle for less. The conflict may not be in our awareness, however, since defences can be built around a pattern, making change more difficult as a consequence.

Childhood experiences or experiences of the past may not be remembered as such. We have an *affective memory*, however, whereby past likes and dislikes can continue to influence us, even without our being aware of them. Automatic reactions to people or events in life illustrate this: likes or dislikes at first sight, reacting to people as if they were parents or siblings, a tendency to categorise all authority figures in the same way. It does not have to be a traumatic event that leads to repression – a repeated pattern of 'small' events can lead to the same result; encountering repeated rejection in little ways can add up to persistent self-doubt. Events that are 'forgotten' can come back later; patterns can repeat themselves in life and in relationships.

When a pattern is tied to the past, it tends to restrict openness to change. In that case, it becomes more difficult to experience the current situation as new rather than a continuation of the past in some form or other. This can manifest itself as resistance, or lack of openness, where an unacceptable emotion is not allowed expression or may not be permitted to enter into awareness. Something from the past can be influencing what is being experienced now and how it is being dealt with. This can lead to the avoidance of a new situation that may be conducive to growth. The inward journey is ongoing and is key to growth in self-discovery and freedom. It is true, however, that all is not clear to us in many situations, since the unconscious exists and has its influence.

Growth in human development involves movement. The resolution of one stage can become the 'problem' in the next. For example, a child has to bond with the mother in the first months of life, though later the task will be to separate, and then to individuate, to form a personal identity.

Whatever approach is taken, it is clear that where there is development or movement there are milestones. Given that one enters life in a dependent state, and that affect dominates in early life until parents put some restrictions on it, there is a challenge to let go of one's own way. Some of the following are indicators of growth: a movement from 'poor me' to a better sense of self; from dependence and/or independence to mutuality; from anger to conviction; from fear to trust; from sexuality (lust) to intimacy (love). By reflecting on our life choices, our faith perspective and the influences that come from the past, we can note the quality of the adaptation and changes we have made in our own lives.

Level of Human Development and Prayer

Psychology and theories of development help us to know and accept ourselves, and to change in the light of the values we hold. Belief in God and in Gospel values adds a further dimension and offers a different vision. Relationship with the Lord, involving prayer and reflection, gives us a greater incentive to grow in freedom of response with a further goal in mind. We are invited to appropriate the past and have some project for the future. What we discover about ourselves in all of this can either confirm or disturb us: it can affirm our gifts or challenge our selfishness, or both. Awareness is important and makes change possible. Life is a journey of discovery, and when we cease to be surprised we have ceased to live. For that reason, development does not cease, but is an ongoing process. Being more at home with ourselves, with others and with the Lord is something that goes on throughout life. It takes time and freedom for this to happen.

The level of our human development has its influence on how we pray, for it is the same person who prays and who also relates to others. How we see ourselves and God, and how we experience life, influences our prayer. Our image of God can move on from a childhood one, or it can remain rather fixed. Good experiences are beneficial, just as past hurts or expectations can continue to influence us. Guilt for not measuring up to our own expectations or those of significant others can remain.

Trust is basic to prayer and to our relationship with ourselves, with others and with God. It can grow through a lessening of fear, although fear can sometimes continue to dominate in our lives, or in certain areas of our lives. Unconscious factors can be influential, and old patterns can remain unless awareness leads to more freedom. Psychologists talk of making the unconscious conscious, thereby making choice possible. Freedom is needed to move on. Lack of freedom can manifest itself in different ways – in resistance, for example, or by putting an interpretation learned later as an adult on a childhood event. This can lead to guilt, even in situations where the child was blameless.

We live our lives in relationship – with ourselves, with others, with the world around us, and with God. Significant for those relationships is the degree of freedom we have, as well as the fears that may restrict them. Prayer is a *relationship* with the Lord, who calls each of us to the fullness of our vocation. It implies a relationship where both parties are active: God invites and we are to respond. *Relating to God* calls for an active disclosing of self, an openness and presence to God. Prayer is learned by praying: it is *a lived experience*, a skill acquired by being led by the Lord in doing it. Freedom tends to grow as the Lord takes over, moving us from obligation to something more interior, to an inner law written on our hearts (Jeremiah 31:33). It is more than an exercise to be performed, since it touches our relationships with the Lord, others and ourselves. What we do subjectively is guided by what the Lord reveals and asks. God's desires meet ours and transform them, as happened to the Samaritan Woman (John 4). She wanted water, but the Lord desired living water for her. Initially, her bucket was a prized possession, but in the end she went home without it.

Over time, as freedom grows, prayer tends to move to the heart. It becomes a prayer of presence, of surrender and of openness to the loving action of God. Fewer words are needed, since it involves a relationship beyond words, images or ideas. Life is seen and experienced differently: more gratitude for God's goodness is present, and emptiness or failure may be experienced as creating space for God rather than providing an occasion for self-recrimination. With growing openness and receptivity to what the Lord offers, a different approach begins to emerge.

While we may be strong and open in some areas, there may be other areas where we are vulnerable, sometimes without our knowing it, and where our capacity to listen and to respond can be restricted or blocked. While we grow in freedom, there may be areas where we resist freedom too. Prayer can increase our freedom and bring healing of the past. While facilitating a better relationship with a loving God, prayer can also strengthen our belief in ourselves and in the fact that we are lovable.

Whenever we enter a new situation with openness, something will emerge. Prayer draws us into the mystery of God and opens out the mystery of our own lives too, where there is freedom to receive the gift of God. Patterns of life and experiences of the past will surface. Some will evoke gratitude, while others will invite us to let go and move into greater freedom. If there is no movement at all, something is missing. As we meditate on the life and values of Christ, we will tend to be *moved* in some way – inspired by his example, perhaps, or strengthened by his courage, or held back by blocks, fears and doubts. We may not be able to understand the experience by ourselves, and we may need to take it to someone else who can help us interpret it and discern what is going on. A spiritual director can facilitate the appreciation of our gifts, and also draw our attention to where we are called to be more open to the invitation of God.

Human Dialectic
It helps us to understand that, as human beings, we are pulled in different directions; there is a struggle within each of us between generous and selfish responses (Romans 7:14–21). Like a struggle between light and darkness, there is a basic imbalance in our hearts, with different elements wrestling with each other. Our decisions are often influenced by different factors, and our motivation is often not very clear. Indeed, our motivation is frequently mixed, as we try to serve God and meet our own needs at the same time, but often we are unaware of the ambiguity. For example, giving alms to the poor is clearly enjoined by the Gospel, but it can be a means of making the giver feel better, too. Moving forward is not something that happens automatically, but freedom is essential if we are to grow. The level of freedom that is present can be manifested in our prayer, and will tend to raise two issues:

- The goodness and mystery of God and what *draws us* to this;
- Our own frailty, unsureness and creaturehood, which can either *open us* to a greater sense of God's wonder, or it can lead us to *resist* it. We can be *blocked* to growth and change. We can resist seeing ourselves as we really are and be unduly critical, or we can tend to see God as made in our own image and likeness. Blind spots, prejudices and resistance are facts of life and exercise their influence.

Both of these factors – being drawn and being 'held back', or being drawn and being driven – are part of life and prayer. There is the tendency to 'do it my way', to seek the easier route, or to remain in control. All of this reveals the image of God and the image of the self that are present, and both of these indicate the quality of the relationship involved, and how well prayer relates to life.

We are drawn by the Lord, although there may not be an immediate response to the Lord's invitation. Some resistance is to be expected, and frequently we have to deal with it to facilitate our moving on. This entails coming to know the Lord and ourselves better. It is what happened to the chosen people on their journey in Exodus, and what occurred in the lives of Jesus' disciples as he moved towards Jerusalem. They had to become more free if they were to continue on the journey with him and to move at his pace. On that journey, they were challenged to let go of their own ways and expectations, and that proved to be a struggle for them.

When the challenge comes to let go of our own way, many people do not find it easy to accept the emotional struggle it involves and to bring it to God. For example, we can experience resistance to anger, to sexuality or to fear, as if these were inappropriate. Some people need to be helped to understand that emotions are part of life: they do not choose to feel them, but they can choose what they do with them. Anger can arise at something that happens, a new situation may invoke fear, or a new opportunity may cause excitement, but the feeling does not have to decide the outcome. It is for the individual to choose the direction taken.

The above-mentioned situations are to be taken to prayer and they call for reflection. There are passages in Scripture that may help. Jeremiah (20:7–8) and Job (3:1–14) were not happy with their situations or how God was dealing with them, but they stated how they felt. The Psalms frequently give expression to distressing emotions and struggles (for example Psalms 22, 38, 51, 88, 129, 130). Human struggles are taken to the Lord. When the Lord is seen as a friend, one who desires what is best, it is easier to bring struggle and resistance to prayer. It is worth reiterating that it is not the existence of emotions that is important, but what we choose to do with them. For example, anger gives life when it can be well directed, as we see when the Lord was angry with the buyers and sellers in the Temple (John 2:13–22). Paul, the energetic persecutor of the Church, did not become wishy-washy following his conversion, but directed his energy in a new way. He did not remain a prisoner of the past, as his earlier resistance gave way to a new calling and response.

Resistance can show up in prayer itself, but it can also be suggested by the passages of Scripture that are chosen or avoided. (This will be dealt with more fully in Chapter 8.) At times, we want and we do not want, and we may try to hide from the latter. We tend to protect ourselves, building defensive walls around our frailties. As well as its gifts, life has its vulnerabilities, but the latter can be opportunities for opening up, when the light gets in through the cracks. If we ever claim to have it all together, presenting ourselves as always right and never admitting failure, we are portraying ourselves as having arrived at our goal and not needing God. This is not the reality.

All people use defences, so it can be helpful to note the type of defences that are operative in life and in prayer. We can think of the Pharisee in the Temple ('Thank God I am not like the rest of humankind'), or of the problem encountered by the rich young man. When certain defences are used too much, they indicate some difficulty, some resistance. The truth about ourselves and about God challenges us, but it is ordered to healing and liberation. It means coming to accept that we are loved sinners in relationship with a loving God who wants what is best for us. We may have to get beyond a defensive stance for that to happen, if we are to see and accept the naked truth about ourselves and to be more in touch with a loving, creative God. We can be blocked by many factors: our sinfulness, the fear of being drawn by the Lord, the fear of too much being asked of us. We can be restricted both in the *giving* and *receiving* of love. We can resist our gifts too, or fail to acknowledge them, but they are God's gifts to us, to be used for God's glory.

Growth in Life and Prayer

Growth, or some movement, is an indication of life and change. In a reflective life, our prayer and our relationship with the Lord undergo some transformation. This may appear as a movement from self-reliance (pride) to reliance on God who is faithful. There is a basic shift of attention from self to the Lord. It can begin like the 'if only' that the woman of Samaria hears the Lord speak (John 4:10). It will probably be followed by many 'yes buts' before a deeper 'yes' is reached. Growth in the Lord involves a movement: from 'poor me' to genuine humility (which is based on the truth and is open); from finding an identity to having an identity in Christ; from unhealthy guilt to true guilt; from loneliness to solitude; from independence to dependence on God; from control to surrender, from my way to God's way; from my kingdom to God's Kingdom.

We can talk of growth and development in terms of *knowing self, accepting self* and *changing self*. Psychology and theories of human development facilitate this; they help us to get in touch with our gifts and to understand where our freedom is restricted, thereby opening up possibilities for us to move on. It is important for us to believe that change is possible, and that in the context of our faith change is ultimately towards Christ. He becomes the focus and his values point the way. We desire to move in the direction he indicates, but we know from experience that growth usually takes place slowly, often in fits and starts; we seldom encounter miracles or quick radical change.

Central for us as believers is a view of the human person as created in love and for love, capable of growing in relationship with the Lord. We believe also that God is active in our lives, and that we can take hold of what God communicates to us, growing in our response as trust deepens. By acknowledging that we are creatures, and that we can misuse our freedom, we are led to deepen our need for healing and liberation in relationship with a loving God who forgives. Leaving home and going his own way helped the Prodigal to come to his senses and return home. Turning to our faithful God helps us be more open to the ongoing adventure of life, where hope is clearly present. Our faithful God promises what we need. The challenge for us is to be open and receptive to the good gifts that are offered.

What is written above is also true for those we accompany on the journey of life. They have their own story and their own invitation from the Lord – to move on, and to grow in freedom and response. Helping them to become aware of their deeper gifts, and of the areas where they may be blind or unaware, can facilitate further growth in freedom in their relationships with the Lord and with others.

Reflection

Where do you notice growth that has been significant in your life?
What does your choice of Scripture for prayer tell you about yourself and your call?

Chapter 4

Gospel Call to the Human Person

Life is a formative journey, and background influences are significant in it. When a faith perspective is taken into account, the goals of life are clear, since they come from the Lord. The Gospel call makes little sense unless we are capable of engaging with it and responding to it. This means that we have the ability to grow and change, and are called beyond our past. Believing that we are called into relationship with God provides a new horizon and an ultimate goal to life. Nevertheless, while we desire to respond more fully to the invitation of the Lord, we remain limited human beings. We need to understand ourselves and the Lord more fully so that this relationship can develop and grow. There are several factors that can deepen our understanding of ourselves and our call in the light of the Gospel.

We are indebted to the insights of psychology in coming to a better understanding of the human person. Psychology has shed much light on human motivation and on how the inner working of a person finds an outer expression in life. Many different psychological theories offer their own contribution to an understanding of the human person. Some of these theories pay greater attention to a particular dimension – the behavioural, the affective or the rational – while others offer a combination of these. The variety of approaches affirms the giftedness of the human person, the mystery of human life, and the complexity of the human journey. Knowing the self more fully and growing in freedom are integral to all of them. The degree of attention given to the unconscious varies considerably, as does the significance attributed to it. An insight into these factors can be gained by looking at the forms of therapy or counselling that are offered to facilitate growth in human freedom. Here psychological theory comes down to reality in the life of a person, the quality of their life and relationships, and the level of their commitment.

By and large, psychological approaches remain at the secular level, without bringing God into the framework. Some are opposed to religion, seeing it as part of the problem, an attempt to escape from reality rather than being immersed in it. Religion, in this view, is too other-worldly in its focus, not concentrating sufficiently on the reality of this world with its issues. Other approaches are more open to religious belief. Without adopting any clear stand on it, they take the position that whatever helps, including faith, can be taken on board. What is common is that the majority of psychologists stay at the secular level, and see the goals of life, such as freedom in some form or other, arising from the person. What the freedom is for remains at the human level also.

For the majority of psychological approaches, the goals of life arise from within ourselves or within the group. Thus, great significance is attached to our personal vision and to what is socially acceptable. Finding ourselves and being more comfortable in ourselves and in our relationships with others are important aspects. Psychologists will speak of growth in self-knowledge and self-acceptance, resulting in greater freedom. How this freedom is lived or expressed will depend on our vision of life and the values that we cherish. Understandably, the goals remain at the human level, since these approaches do not set out to include God or the religious dimension.

Psychology has a valuable contribution to make in helping us to further our self-knowledge and freedom. It can help us to understand ourselves and the influences in our lives, so that we are more free to move onwards. With a greater appreciation of our gifts, and more freedom to deal with what can restrict us, new opportunities can be seized and new avenues opened. Through these insights, the Lord can invite us to draw closer, calling us to more faithful imitation.

Some Psychological Contributions

It may be helpful at this point to look at a few different psychological approaches, and acknowledge their contributions and their limitations. What is offered below is selective, but it serves to indicate some different factors that may foster our understanding of the human person who responds to the call of the Lord. Each theory presents a view of the person and how growth and freedom might be fostered. Some of the theories, not seeing great potential for change, could be classified as more pessimistic or negative in tone; these tend to give more attention to the past and to unconscious influences. Others, giving less attention to the unconscious and seeing greater scope for change, are more optimistic or positive. The following models, while not pretending to be comprehensive, may help our reflection.

- There are models that see human life from the perspective of conflict, whether the conflict is primarily within the person or with others. Life then becomes a form of compromise between the different tensions and conflicts involved. This approach tends to have a more negative view of the human person and of life. More attention is given to past experience and to unconscious influences, with limited freedom to change radically envisaged.
- In contrast, self-fulfilment theories take a more positive view, seeing life largely in terms of realising one's potential. The person is good and needs the right environment for the blueprint to unfold in a healthy way. This approach speaks of love and unconditional positive regard. Overall, it has an optimistic perspective, with more attention being given to the present, and greater freedom for change accepted. To some people it is too optimistic, leading to high expectations that cannot be met.
- Another viewpoint is that of Viktor Frankl, who spoke of the search for meaning as central. Frankl, a Jewish psychiatrist, was imprisoned in a concentration camp during the Second World War. From his own observation of how some prisoners gave up hope in the camps, while others saw reason to live, he recognised the importance of

freedom and meaning in life. Having survived this situation of extreme conflict, he wrote of a search for meaning, and how the human has the capacity to choose, even in extreme situations where there was little scope for external choice. It is possible to choose an attitude towards a situation that one cannot change outwardly.

Frankl lived in a situation of great conflict, externally and internally, but was able to come through it because he had the will to do so. While recognising the value of the self-fulfilment approach, he also saw its limits, claiming that in order to be fulfilled you had to aim at something else. You could not aim at happiness itself, he pointed out, so you had to do something that would bring happiness. The same applied to self-fulfilment, he argued: you could not aim at it directly. Thus, Frankl spoke of the need for self-transcendence as the goal that can bring self-fulfilment as a by-product. You transcend yourself to fulfil yourself. For Frankl, meaning and values are more than what arises from the individual, for they need an objective quality to bring about true self-fulfilment. Frankl saw the need for some goal beyond the self as necessary for meaning in life. The goals of life he envisaged, however, did not go beyond the human level. So, while Frankl moves us a stage further than the conflict and self-fulfilment models, the goals still remain within the human or secular level.

The Gospel Call
Conflict, self-fulfilment and self-transcendence: these models can offer us a basis from which to look at our call in following the Lord, and at what happens when we include the Lord in the framework. Within a restricted vision, they help portray the human situation and indicate its potential. In one form or another, however, the human or secular level remains their measure. It is different when the goals of life arise from the Lord, calling us to something more than the secular level. The Christian approach serves to enlarge the horizon and to give other reasons for living in a particular way. It acknowledges the same basics of human life – dealing with conflict, living in relationships and searching for meaning – but we are presented with a

different horizon when we begin with God.

The Christian perspective, then, acknowledges the human and secular levels, but it goes further. These levels exist and are part of life, but they do not fully define it. They provide a basis for further discussion and offer relevant helps, but we need more. We can fruitfully draw on elements of all of the above models, since each contains a truth. For example, St Paul speaks of the struggle and inner conflict a person experiences, pulled in different directions (Romans 7:14–25). We know too that conflicts of different kinds exist around the world – political, social and economic – and that sometimes these struggles take place in the name of God.

We live in relationships, and in order to have stability and security we desire some level of meaning and consistency just as we seek to be fulfilled. In our desire for peace and contentment, we can find help in Frankl's approach, but we can also bring it a step further. In the light of our faith and our call to be servants of Jesus and his message, we can move beyond Frankl's understanding of self-transcendence at a merely human level. Jesus is our reason for self-transcendence. The call is to transcend the self in and for Christ. It is his message, his example, his values and his call that inspire us to move onwards and guide us on the journey. We fulfil ourselves and realise our potential by living for Christ, by going beyond ourselves and our own interests and concerns.

Beginning with God brings with it a very different perspective. It acknowledges the existence of conflict and the need for compromise on occasion, just as it acknowledges God's desire for us to come to the fullness of life, but it sets about achieving it in a different manner. We know that we are created in the image of God, and are called to praise, reverence and serve God. God is present and active in our lives, and has shared good gifts with us. God's invitation to us is to live in that spirit, so that transcending ourselves is inherent in who we are as children of God. Going beyond ourselves means looking to Jesus in the Gospel as the criterion for living. Reaching out to others arises from our relationship with God, who reaches out to us. Serving others is serving Christ in them. Our motivation is to be Jesus-centred.

Change in ourselves, then, means to be set free for Christ, and not just for our own sake. Jesus' life was lived for others, including us, and this gives us a specific reason to go beyond ourselves and to be persons for him and for others. His self-giving in death was life-giving for us. His call to us is to go beyond, to give more, to forgive, even to love our enemies (Matthew 5:43–38). We are reminded that it is in giving that we receive, and that it is in dying to ourselves we are set free and find life (see, for example, John 12:24–25). It is by losing life that we find it.

In the Incarnation, Jesus entered the human story with all its gifts and limitations. The people he called were not necessarily the brightest or the best. The choosing of the twelve apostles would leave the modern human resources expert somewhat baffled. Few of the twelve seemed very promising in human terms, and several of them would not have had good psychological profiles. Peter was impulsive, James and John were ambitious, Thomas was sceptical. And what about Judas? Did Jesus make a mistake in choosing him?

The apostles' call was a call *from*, a call *to* and a call *for* something more than themselves and their own interests. It was a call to trust God, but to recognise that God trusted them first. It was God who began the good work and who would see it through to completion (Philippians 1:6). Their call was more about what God could do through them than what they themselves could do.

Personal Response

There are different approaches to life, as there are different approaches to spirituality. They can be negative or positive in tone, and they can be problem-centred or gift-oriented. Each human story has its gifts and its complexities, its ups and downs and its hopes and aspirations for the future. Living in a fast-changing world with rapid communications provides opportunities and challenges that influence the quality of the decisions we make. These decisions cover a wide spectrum, from personal choices to choices made about relationships, work, the environment and the future. How we see life and what we want from it are influenced by many factors, from within and without. Information can be beneficial, but it needs to be processed.

Self-knowledge can help us have the internal resources to choose well. Processing the past is important in discarding excess baggage and travelling more lightly into the future. Where we begin our story says much about us, while the approach we take to life involves a further revelation. Our approach can be too negative, too positive or finely balanced. What we have learnt from our life experience is an indication of our reflective capacity. Psychological and spiritual approaches can help in all of this. However, while they may have similar starting points – looking at life and finding the self – they will have different points of arrival, since the spiritual includes God in the story.

We are in relationship with God who calls us to holiness, to the fullness of life. Holiness is not to be confused with wholeness or with psychological health. It means that we use the freedom we have, no matter how great or limited it may be, in love. God's call is to grow in freedom, to acknowledge the gifts that are present and to allow them to be developed further and put to good use. The light is not to be put under a bushel but to give glory to God and hope to others.

We are called into relationship with Jesus and to be people for others. We are called to transcend the self for Christ. That is true for each of us, no matter how gifted or limited we may be. In Jesus, the divine and the human met, and we pray to share in the divinity of the one who humbled himself to share our humanity. Where the divine meets the human there is transformation: the ordinary meets the extraordinary. This relationship with God enhances our dignity, our origin and our destiny, and gives a further reason to respect others who are also children of God.

The goals set before us do not arise from ourselves. They are not a human invention, or arrived at by some form of consensus. They are from God. They are beyond ourselves, and are to be found in the life, teaching and values of Jesus. In this way, the horizon moves beyond the secular to the sacred, although the two are intertwined for us. The vision is grounded in reality, but it is full of hope because it acknowledges the freedom to change. The call is to incarnate Jesus now.

The scriptural vision of life – with its goals and values, its understanding of what the human person is created for, and why – provides a perspective on life and relationships that is different from the secular. It acknowledges the psychological insights, but it takes us a step further by widening the vision. This enlarged horizon gives us a clear set of values to guide our life and relationships. It does not forget that we are human, that we are gifted but limited. It takes into account that we lose direction, but assures us that God calls and welcomes us back.

We are made for transcendence and capable of it: this is an important background consideration for understanding and responding to our call. God's invitation is not in any way alien to who we are; rather, it recognises our dignity and that God is within us already and sharing love with us. God then invites us further, to share more fully in that life in love. God's call is an acknowledgement of our potential. God trusts us to respond, and calls for our trust in turn. The invitation points to the future, and to the ultimate goal of life – being with God.

Jesus was fully aware of the human situation, with its gifts and limitations. In calling for conversion of heart, Jesus acknowledged the inner conflict. By advocating reconciliation, he recognised the conflict that exists with others. In offering life to the full, he acknowledged the desire for fulfilment. By his own self-giving love to the end, he demonstrated how this was attained. He showed that being truly human, as he was, did not mean that we are limited to the secular level; rather, he reminded us of our true dignity as children of God who are called to the fullness of life with him forever.

When our call is seen in this light, we see how it is addressing the gift within and enabling that gift to flourish. Drawing honey from the flower does not destroy the flower or its beauty, but it spreads richness around it. Similarly, we are called to offer life to others. God respects our freedom but knows our potential, and desires to bring it to fruition. Call and response fit into the framework of God's plan for us.

Growth and formation often have to deal with human limitations rather than faith. We know, however, that God can work through human limitations, for Jesus called ordinary people as his companions, and clay jars can hold the precious treasure (2 Corinthians 4:7). Human frailty can lead us to be open to the gift of God. Jesus' life and teachings, with their joys and challenges, point the way for his followers, so that the choices we make are to be guided by this orientation and relationship. While psychology provides a good basic structure for understanding the human person, it can leave dormant or undeveloped a whole other aspect of life with its rich potential. The deeper gift can remain unwrapped and not appreciated.

There are limits to human freedom, but we can grow. While acknowledging unconscious influences, the call is to be led and formed by the Lord, incarnating love, joy and hope and immersing ourselves in life as he did. It is an invitation to be a disciple of Jesus.

Reflection

Psychology offers aids to finding ourselves.
What is the relevance of this?
How do you understand losing self to find self?

Chapter 5

Discipleship

Every leader offers a vision to others, whether in political, social or religious matters. We need a vision in life to provide direction, to give an incentive for growth, to call us onwards. Without vision we lose direction (see Proverbs 29:18, sometimes translated as 'without vision the people perish'). That was true for the chosen people, though their vision was not always very clear, becoming blurred at times by external and internal factors. This reminds us that there are different goals on offer, different visions for life, and different means to living them.

The vision may involve following someone, choosing a way of life, being involved in a movement or committed to a cause – or it might be a combination of all these. Whether it involves a long-term commitment, or is tied to a particular event, such as an election campaign, it will entail some giving of self. Believing in something or being committed to someone, with the investment of time and energy involved, is part of life. This reality can be seen to be present in widely different circumstances. For example, in the book *Wild Swans* by Jung Chang, we read the story of three generations of women in China. Centred on the mother, who was a committed follower of Mao, the book illustrates what that meant, the many challenges involved, and the loyalty and commitment that was expected and tested many times. The followers of Mother Teresa, in her service of the poor, or of Nelson Mandela, with his new vision for South Africa, can serve as other examples.

Out of concern for family, Church, human rights, the environment or political causes, people commit themselves to others and to the vision they espouse. They are called beyond themselves by some desired vision, value system and goal. The level of desire and energy invested is a significant indicator of the quality of the commitment. Being half-interested does little to energise a person to make a choice or to take decisive action. Each decision we make implies a choice: by opting for something, we forego the alternative. Clear choices give direction to life, both in what we choose and in what we give up.

Called by Name
Being called by God for some particular mission is part of our faith story. Abram and Sarai were called to come into a new land and form a new people (Genesis 12). God would be faithful to his promise, as affirmed in God's message to Jacob, 'Know that I am with you and will keep you wherever you go' (Genesis 28:15). In fulfilment of this promise, many people were called to a special relationship with God and to leadership within the community. God called Moses to lead the people out of slavery in Egypt, promising to be with him (Exodus 3). David was chosen as king and anointed (1 Samuel 16). As we read in the book called after her, there was a significant role for Ruth in God's plan, as there was for Deborah as a judge (Judges 4) and for Judith as a leader (Judith 8). The prophetic message of the Old Testament and the call to leadership of certain people provide a good foundation in faith for what happened with the coming of Jesus as Messiah and Saviour.

The New Testament builds on the Old. Jesus called people to be disciples, companions for mission. By his proclamation of the Kingdom, he gave them a vision. He introduced himself in prophetic terms, presenting himself in continuity with the past while offering something radically new: 'Do not think that I have come to abolish the law or the prophets; I have come not to abolish, but to fulfil' (Matthew 5:17). At the beginning of his mission Jesus called people to be his companions: 'He went up the mountain and called to him those whom he wanted, and they came to him. And he appointed twelve, whom he also named apostles, to be with him, and to be sent out to proclaim the message, and to have authority to cast out demons' (Mark 3:13–19).

It is clear that it was the Lord's initiative and choice to call them by name. They were chosen to proclaim the good news and to bring healing, but their call involved an internal dimension as well as an external one. Externally, they were to have a role in Jesus' mission, with tasks to do. The internal dimension was important, however, for they were to be companions, people who knew Jesus and had a personal relationship with him. They were to be formed in his way of thinking and being, which would involve a change of heart.

The initial response of the first disciples was generous, as they left all to follow Jesus. That generosity was important in enabling them to embark on the journey. At that early stage, the external dimension was evident in the way they left behind boats, tax booths and the people they worked with. In time, however, the internal aspect would become more pronounced, as their own desires, interests, expectations, fears and concerns became more prominent, and the implications of what following Jesus actually entailed became clearer. We can see, then, that while the call involved an initial moment of decision, the decision was actually ongoing in reality, because the invitation to grow in response to the call was always there. Within the existing call, there would be further invitations specifying how it was to be lived out. All of this meant that the relationship with the Lord could deepen.

Jesus set about forming those he called as disciples, giving them his 'mission statement' in the Beatitudes (Matthew 5:1–12). Here, they learned that blessedness would be found in a surprising way, very different from that of the world. By being with Jesus as he proclaimed the good news of the Kingdom and healed the sick, his disciples had practical learning opportunities. They were like apprentices, learning from what Jesus taught and also from his example. Nevertheless, they were slow to understand the call, to know Jesus and to understand what he was about. In the gospels, faith in Jesus was often weaker in his chosen ones than in other, frequently surprising, people. The strong faith of the centurion (Matthew 8:5–13) and the Canaanite woman (Matthew 15:21–28) was in marked contrast to the little faith of the disciples at the storm at sea (Matthew 8:26) or in their failed attempt to cast out a demon (Matthew 17:20). Believing in Jesus is a prominent theme throughout the Gospel of John (for example John 5:24; 6:40, 47), and belief in Jesus is summarised as the purpose of this gospel: 'These are written so that you may come to believe that Jesus is the Messiah, the Son of God, and that through believing you may have life in his name' (John 20:31). Many people struggled with this faith, including the disciples, but Jesus never gave up on them despite their failures, their frailty and their self-concern. Although in many ways they were slow learners, Jesus continued to teach them and invite them onwards, never leaving them where they were.

Ordinary people were called from their everyday work to be disciples of Jesus. Their call did not begin from a place of perfection, but came in the midst of life. The ideal of a new relationship with God and with others invited them onwards but, while the disciples had their own gifts, they were also weak and limited. They were the 'earthen vessels' that held the treasure (2 Corinthians 4:7), wounded healers who would minister to others in the Lord's name. The reality is that they were called, though they were sinners. The Lord who shared our human nature reminded them that their limitations were not to dominate. Fear was not to prevail, as is made clear in several texts involving call (for example Luke 1:26–38; Matthew 14:22–33). Throughout Scripture, those called in a special way – Isaiah (Isaiah 6:1–10), Jeremiah (Jeremiah 1:4–10), Peter (Luke 5:1–11), Paul (1 Timothy 1:12–17) – did not think themselves worthy, protesting their unsuitability. The call was not merited, nor was it earned; it was God's gift, given for God's purpose. Sometimes a new name was given, implying a special mission of some kind. This was evident as Abram was renamed Abraham, Jacob became Israel, Simon became Peter, and Saul became Paul.

While discipleship is often envisaged in terms of action, Jesus also calls for change within. That call is ongoing, as we have seen. Growth in freedom to respond is part of the faith journey. The Lord knew of the capacity of the disciples to grow in love, and for that reason he did not leave them where they were. They were invited onwards, despite their weakness of faith and their many failures. The Lord was committed to them and was patient with them. He proclaimed to his disciples a kingdom of justice, love and truth that would bring inner peace. His fundamental message was love of God and neighbour. For this he recognised the need for conversion of heart, leading to action undertaken with the right motivation of giving glory to God (Matthew 6:1–18). Lip service, or mouthing the right words, was inadequate (Matthew 15:1–9; 23:2–3). Inner conversion was to find an outer expression in life, providing it with a solid base. For the disciples, coming to accept this message was a slow process.

Women Disciples

For much of the Gospel story, attention is paid to the chosen twelve and their response. We see their struggle, resistance and blindness as Jesus tried to form them. In these accounts, however, it is easy to miss the fact that there were some women who played a prominent role, often behind the scenes, in Jesus' public life. His friends Martha and Mary welcomed him into their home (Luke 10:38–42). Other women followed him on his missionary journey to Jerusalem. This is mentioned in Matthew and Mark, but it is stated more clearly in Luke where we read that Jesus 'went on through cities and villages, proclaiming and bringing the good news of the kingdom of God. The twelve were with him, as well as some women who had been cured of evil spirits and infirmities: Mary, called Magdalene, from whom seven demons had gone out, and Joanna, the wife of Herod's steward Chuza, and Susanna, and many others, who provided for them out of their resources' (Luke 8:1–3).

Some significant details should be noted in that brief account:
- There were women who accompanied Jesus and the apostles on the mission.
- Some of them had been cured, suggesting that their healing had led to their decision to follow him.
- Some of them were named, but there were also *many others*.
- The women provided for Jesus and the apostles out of their own resources. (Perhaps they were better off than most others at the time. In any case, their generosity in sharing what they had allowed them to care for Jesus and facilitate his mission.)

The passage speaks of the inclusion of women in the mission. It tells us of their faith, and their generosity in providing for Jesus and the apostles. These women showed fidelity in the ordinary things, whereas the apostles often seemed more interested in the extraordinary.

Providing for Jesus and the twelve out of their resources was not something that happened just once. It is clear that these women became followers of Jesus and were part of his missionary group. Later, we are reminded that the women who had followed Jesus from Galilee were present at his crucifixion. We are told that 'all his acquaintances, including the women who had followed him from Galilee, stood at a distance, watching these things' (Luke 23:49).

These women remained behind when the crowds who had gathered for the spectacle had gone home: 'The women who had come with him from Galilee followed, and they saw the tomb and how his body was laid' (Luke 23:55). This brief reference tells us that these women, having been faithful followers of Jesus all along, remained with him for his burial. Loyal to the end, they were the last to leave the tomb. Where were the apostles at this time? They seem to have left the scene. Matthew tells us that they deserted and fled when Jesus was arrested (Matthew 26:56). The men have vanished from sight, while three women are explicitly named from among several others who were present: 'Now it was Mary Magdalene, Joanna, Mary the mother of James, and the other women with them who told this to the apostles' (Luke 24:10).

Continuing their love and service, in their desire to anoint the body of Jesus the women were also the first to arrive at the tomb when the sabbath was over. They knew where Jesus had been buried, but when they came to the tomb they found the stone rolled back and the tomb empty. Running back to share their experience, they became apostles to the apostles.

Those women were faithful followers from Jesus' time in Galilee. They were willing to stay with him in his suffering. They were present at his crucifixion, and they were ready to risk going to the tomb at first light on the sabbath. They became witnesses to the resurrection.

The following points should be noted:
- The women had seen Jesus being buried, so they knew where the tomb was. The twelve did not.
- Having come to the tomb, the women were perplexed by the unexpected scene, wondering what it meant. Different explanations were possible, but they were told what it signified: 'He is not here, but has risen' (Luke 24:5).
- Jesus' story, which was already familiar to the women, was now revealed to them in a new light: 'Remember how he told you while he was still in Galilee ... then they remembered his words' (Luke 24:6–8). They came to see that the prediction of his passion, death and resurrection had been fulfilled.
- Already identified as followers of Jesus in Galilee (Luke 8:2–3), Mary Magdalene and Joanna are named among the women returning from the tomb (Luke 24:10). They had clearly followed Jesus all along the way from Galilee to Jerusalem.
- The women went to the apostles to tell them what they had found and heard.
- At first, the women's story was rejected by the apostles, who considered it an idle tale.

For these women, the road from Galilee to Jerusalem was an internal as well as an external journey. They had followed Jesus all along the way, showing love, faith, service and fidelity to the end of his life. They then became witnesses to the resurrection. That is the call for each disciple.

Response to the Call

These women were faithful followers. They show how people came to faith in Jesus in different ways, some through being healed and others through hearing and seeing. For all of them, it meant coming to an inner conviction beyond external events. The call to commitment and service in love remains the invitation. Some people were able to stay with Jesus, while others could not accept his teaching or stay with him in his suffering. Discipleship calls us beyond ourselves, allowing the Lord to work through us and knowing that this involves more than human effort. St Paul put the focus on the action of God: 'Glory be to him whose power working in us can do infinitely more than we can ask or imagine' (Ephesians 3:20–21). It is about being servants as Jesus was, and allowing him to work through us.

Discipleship involves the meeting of two freedoms: the Lord's freedom in calling and our freedom in responding. It recognises that we can change, and that we can respond more generously. Growing in inner freedom is central to that journey, but it can involve pain, as we come face to face with the wonderful giftedness God has shared with us as well as with our own limits. We like the gift, but we can be a bit uneasy with it, like Moses in the presence of the burning bush (Exodus 3:1–6), or the three apostles at the scene of the Transfiguration (Matthew 17:1–8). We can grow in our awareness of the mystery of God's ways and of our own capacity to respond, but there can be growing pains as we move through and beyond our limits too. We can be held back by our selfishness and frailty, by our ambiguous motivation, and by our blindness to many aspects of our own lives and to the cost of discipleship. Life has its surprises, some joyful and others painful. As partakers in the Paschal Mystery, we have the capacity to follow Jesus through sorrow to joy.

Cost and Rewards of Discipleship
Growing in the Lord's ways is not automatic. It involves struggle and choice. From the beginning, Jesus was presented as a sign of contradiction. Given the prophetic manner of his life and message, people had different reactions and responses to him. Some welcomed him, while others saw him as a threat. The apostles began generously but, as time went on, they were less open to some parts of Jesus' message, especially when he asked them to forego their own interests, or when he spoke of his forthcoming suffering and passion (for example Mark 8:31). The reality is that discipleship costs, as it means putting Jesus and others first. This is challenging, of course, although a lot depends on how we see ourselves and where we seek security and meaning. Following the way of the Lord can lead to emotional suffering: misunderstanding,

criticism, ridicule, being overlooked, misjudged or mistreated. Such emotional suffering was a significant part of Jesus' passion, although we tend to focus more on his physical suffering. Jesus' life was one of passionate love that inspired him to give all in love for us. He reminds us that love needs passion if it is to have depth, but passion needs love if it is to be directed in a life-giving way. Following Jesus involves the internal and the external, which are intertwined in our living as followers of the Lord.

When love predominates, all else is accepted, including love's cost. Lovers cannot do enough for each other, though what they do may make little sense to those observing them. Love involves sacrifice, but much depends on where the emphasis is. If love is the stronger element, the sacrifice is accepted readily; but if sacrifice is the more dominant factor, there will be resentment and frustration.

Jesus drew on his own experience, as well as on that of the prophets, in his self-giving and in alerting his followers to the suffering and persecution they could expect (Matthew 10:17–25; 24:19–24). He called on them to renounce themselves, losing their life in order to find it (Matthew 10:37–39; 16:24–28). He predicted his passion, but the disciples resisted because they were more interested in their own concerns (Matthew 16:21–23; 17:22–23; 20:17–19). In reply to the request of James and John for special places, Jesus invited them to drink the cup that he was going to drink (Mark 10:35–40). His call to the rich young man involved a challenge: 'If you wish to be perfect, go sell your possessions, and give the money to the poor, and you will have treasure in heaven; then come, follow me' (Matthew 19:16–26). Jesus' way was the way of greater love, giving his life for his friends (John 15:13). Dying to the self was the way to new life (John 12:24–25). Jesus' focus was on life and on love, not on the cost involved. He wanted what was best for people.

Discipleship is about having a personal love relationship with Jesus and following him. It is not all about the cost, but rather about the quality of our life with Jesus and with others. Jesus' way was about having love and life to the full, about living as Easter people who share the peace, joy and hope of the resurrection. His predictions of passion and death also foretold the resurrection. His death and resurrection go on in our daily lives, with the ups and down, the joys and sorrows that are part and parcel of life. Discipleship is about life and the fullness of life in God, as promised by Jesus.

Jesus spoke about rewards for being a disciple. Welcoming a prophet or a righteous person would not go unrewarded, nor would a cup of cold water given to a child in the name of a disciple (Matthew 10:40–42). The disciples were blessed because they saw Jesus and heard his message (Matthew 13:16–17). A generous response would be richly rewarded: 'Everyone who has left houses or brothers or sisters or father or mother or children or fields, for my name's sake, will receive a hundredfold, and will inherit eternal life' (Matthew 19:29). Jesus gave reassurance to his followers: 'The harvest is plentiful, but the labourers are few' (Matthew 9:36–38); 'Come to me all you who are weary and are carrying heavy burdens, and I will give you rest' (Matthew 11:28–30). He spoke about attachment to riches, but he also spoke about how all things are possible to God.

Accepting our need of the Incarnation and living by its message are central to being followers of Jesus. He is our good news of salvation, calling us to believe in him and his message as the way to life. Fundamentally, discipleship means committing ourselves, not to a cause, but to a person, Jesus. It is a long-term commitment rather than a passing one. Mary's 'yes' at Nazareth was a foundation for many more to come, including that of Calvary. It was 'yes' to a way of life, to a new relationship. She lived out the commitment she made, and for that reason she is a model disciple for us. We are invited to do the same.

Inner conversion and prayer are basic to our relationship with Jesus, as we seek to fulfil his will and bring about his Kingdom. Jesus told us that discipleship would cost (Matthew 8:18–22) and that there would be persecutions (Matthew 10:16–25), but he also told us to rely on God. That is what Jesus did in his prayer in the garden. His relationship with the Father, as well as his teaching and example, continue to provide direction for us in a time of change and transition. Discipleship has much to do with changing ourselves, although it may also be about changing situations, or others. Jesus' life was one of passionate love, lived out in total self-giving. His life showed that love and passion need each other in a committed life.

Our Call
Our call is to follow Jesus, helping to make him known and loved, and serving him in his mission of bringing good news and healing to today's world. We follow him from birth, through death, to resurrection. Since we follow a person, not just a message, our relationship with him is important if we are to accept his teaching, follow his example and live by his love. He is God-with-us, and our relationship is a personal one. His underlying message today is the same as it was all those years ago, even though we live in a context different from the one in which the Gospel was first presented. Today, we still find the same variety of reactions to Jesus and his message.

Christ's life is the way of the Christian; it is the path to follow. It involves taking on the mind of Christ and following him through each aspect of his mission, including his passion, death and resurrection. He calls us to companionship with him for service to others. His call is always a call away from ourselves, or from what might be called the more selfish side of life. It means going beyond what is convenient in order to be for Christ and for others. Of primary importance is the Lord's invitation, not our own unworthiness. Conversion is at the heart of our following, since it opens us up to the love of God and to the experience of everything as gift, evoking a generous response. Ultimately, a true relationship with Christ seeks to reflect how he expressed love and service.

We are in continuity with people in the Gospel, where conversion often led to discipleship, and where healing frequently prompted the desire to follow (for example Luke 8:1–3; Luke 18:35–43). People who were touched in some way by the Lord entered into a new relationship with him. Their brokenness, their vulnerability and their failures were an opening for the Lord to enter their lives. They were led to the desire to remain with the Lord by recognising the gifts God had shared with them. By acknowledging their true situation (Luke 15:1–3), the people most open to the Lord were those in need, such as the tax collectors and sinners who befriended him. Those who thought they had everything in perfect order were closed to him. They felt they had no need of him, and consequently had no room for him.

We know from Scripture, as well as from life, that the Lord does not call the perfect, but sinners (Mark 2:17). God's vision is bigger than human limitations. We can be too focused on our limitations or our past failures. God seems more concerned with the potential that is present, and sets his sight on offering us a new future. In the great stories of forgiveness in Scripture, such as the Prodigal Son (Luke 15:11–32) or the adulterous woman (John 8:1–11), the past is not the focus.

We are called beyond practical questions and considerations to a different way of being and of relating. Jesus brought his disciples – and others too, such as the woman at the well (John 4:1–30) – beyond the practical to a deeper reality. Much of our following takes place in quiet ways. We provide, serve and are faithful in little ways. Jesus' way is not ostentatious, grandiose or verbose, nor is it the way of Mary or the women of Galilee. We serve in quiet ways by our presence and by how we are with others. The women who followed Jesus seemed to have a greater capacity to accept and live through suffering than the apostles, and they were quicker to believe in the resurrection. No words of theirs are recorded, but they left an eloquent message to us about following Jesus. They were able to stay with him.

The Gospel ends with stories of the resurrection, but discipleship does not end there. In many ways, the apostles' story began in a new way following the resurrection. The coming of the Holy Spirit brought transformation, with everything being experienced in a new light. An inner change took place, making the disciples ready to begin anew without regard to the cost to themselves. A harmony was established between the internal and the external, between the heart and the outer action. The disciples had got the message, literally and metaphorically, and they had the freedom and courage to preach and live it. In reality, as disciples now, we are invited to write the end of the Gospel ourselves, showing how our faith story and our discipleship are in continuity with the faith journey of the first disciples. God remains active in our lives and in our world, and his invitation to come closer never ceases. The personal invitation continues. It is the way of true life and love. Discipleship as a gift is ongoing.

Prayer is important as we grow more fully into discipleship, since it reveals the Lord's desires for us and helps us to accept the transformation being offered. Praying about the Lord's life helps us make our own his vision, goals and attitudes, so that we can be more like him. The Lord does not leave us where we are, since our potential for a loving response can increase. The invitation of the Lord continues as the Lord draws us onwards. Our response is helped by being in touch with the call of the Lord and with our own restless hearts, enabling the desires of the Lord and our own desires to meet more fully. In life, relationships need time and good communication if they are to grow. The same is true of our relationship with the Lord, whose love is constant and faithful.

Reflection

How do you understand discipleship as a call to inner transformation?
What is the relevance of passionate love in the life of Jesus and in that of his disciples?

Chapter 6

Prayer

Prayer is integral to our lives as disciples of the Lord, just as it is to the ministry of spiritual direction and to spiritual discernment. In prayer we are brought into a quieter place in our relationship with the Lord, as it strengthens and guides us in our lives as disciples. Prayer facilitates life and brings integration, enabling us to live more fully in and for the Lord. Prayer and life are brought together when prayer draws from life and feeds back into life.

There are many helpful books available on prayer, suggesting different methods and approaches for different situations and stages of life. Here, I propose to begin with Jesus and the role of prayer in his life. As followers of Jesus we can benefit from looking at his practice of prayer, as well as what he taught about prayer. He is our leader and guide, so his example and his teaching have special importance for us. His prayer tells us about who he was and what he came to be and do. Different aspects are given in the four gospels, with an overall pattern emerging of Jesus as a person of prayer. Looking at some elements of Jesus' practice of prayer helps us in our own prayer and in the ministry of accompanying others on their faith journeys.

Jesus was born into a particular family, culture and faith. He was part of a people with a long and rich faith tradition. Familiarity with Scripture was part of that tradition, particularly the Psalms, the Law and the Prophets. Praying several times each day, including in the morning and at night, was the normal practice for his people. Public worship, such as going to Jerusalem for major festivals and attending the synagogue on the sabbath, was an accepted norm. There is evidence of all of this in the life of Jesus, who went up to

Jerusalem for the festivals, and taught and healed in the synagogue on the sabbath (for example Luke 13:10–17). He frequently quoted from Scripture, claimed that he came to fulfil the Law and the Prophets (Matthew 5:17), and spent time in prayer, getting up early in the morning to pray (Mark 1:35), or spending the whole night in prayer to God (Luke 6:12).

By referring frequently to his practice of prayer, the gospels present Jesus as a person for whom prayer was important. Even at busy times, Jesus could find time for prayer (Matthew 14:23). While he lived in a vibrant Jewish faith culture, the apostles, who were familiar with this tradition, saw that there was something different about his practice of prayer, prompting them to ask him to teach them to pray (Luke 11:1). Having his own unique relationship with the Father, he embodied more than what the tradition gave him. Reverence and praise of the Father, and doing the will of the Father who had sent him, were central for Jesus. Those who grew up with him did not understand him, and were unprepared for the direction his life took (Mark 6:1–3).

Jesus' prayer has relevance for us who are his followers, since we are called to imitate him and to share his life. His practice of prayer has a lot to say to us. It involved a living relationship with the Father, and was clearly linked with the mission he came to accomplish. In the midst of great activity, he had a contemplative presence. On several occasions, his interaction with others brought them into a deeper relationship with him and with the Father, as can be seen, for instance, in the story of the woman at the well, where he led her from her desire for water to his desire for her to have living water (John 4:5–15).

Jesus' Mission and Prayer
These days we tend to give more attention than formerly to the human Jesus, the one who 'increased in wisdom and in years, and in divine and human favour' (Luke 2:52). Jesus was sent by the Father as Saviour. That was his mission. Any attempt to understand him apart from this mission is to lose sight of a key aspect of the meaning of his coming among us. His life was his mission and his mission was his life, not simply part of his life. Jesus grew in

divine and human favour; through a growing awareness of himself and what he was sent to do, he grew into the mission given to him. His relationship with the Father, involving his manifest desire to do the Father's will, gave a clear focus to his prayer and life. That is evident in the gospels from the beginning, as he himself made clear at the finding in the Temple: 'Did you not know that I must be in my Father's house' (Luke 2:49)?

In his commitment to finding and doing his Father's will, and establishing a Kingdom of justice, love and peace, prayer was central to Jesus' life. It could be said that prayer provides a good picture of his mission and that his dedication to mission reveals his prayer life. He sought the Father's will rather than his own, and this was what guided his choices. This is evident from the early stages of Jesus' ministry (for example John 5:30; 6:38), long before the prayer in Gethsemane. His acceptance of the Father's will was an active choice, and not a merely passive submission (John 10:18). Prayer pervaded his life, and was especially evident at key moments as his mission unfolded – at his baptism, at the temptations, at the agony and on the cross. In prayer he found the clarity and strength that enabled him to continue and complete his mission of total self-giving for us.

Jesus' prayer throughout his life gives evidence of a growth in mission. There was a growing desire to do what the Father asked of him and readiness to pay the cost. Several of his sayings – for example, 'My food is to do the will of him who sent me and to complete his work' (John 4:34), and 'I always do what is pleasing to him' (John 8:29) – attest to the depth of his desire. Seeking only the Father's will and glory (John 7:18), Jesus was doing the Father's work and teaching what the Father commanded (John 7:17; 12:49). His will was at one with that of the Father who sent him. His prayer was a discerning prayer, understood in the context of his loving relationship with the Father and his openness to the mission.

That mission gave him energy and enthusiasm: 'I came to bring fire on earth, and how I wish it were already kindled! I have a baptism with which to be baptised, and what stress I am under until it is completed' (Luke 12:49–50). There is great emphasis on Jesus being 'sent', particularly in the

Gospel of John, where it is mentioned more than thirty times. It is from this relationship with the Father who sent him that Jesus drew strength to complete the work he was given to do. Indeed, those works testify to him (John 5:36). He rejoiced in accomplishing his mission: 'I glorified you on earth by finishing the work that you gave me to do' (John 17:4). His life was a journey from 'being about his Father's business' (Luke 2:49) to his final surrender on Calvary: 'Father, into your hands I commend my spirit' (Luke 23:46). Totally open to the Father, he desired to let God's will be the ultimate criterion of his decision: 'Yet, not my will but yours be done' (Luke 22:42).

Jesus' preaching and teaching were nourished by his prayer. His growth in his sense of mission unfolded in an atmosphere of prayer (Luke 5:16), and of a unique and personal relationship with the Father: 'Abba, Father, for you all things are possible' (Mark 14:36). Jesus gave time and space to prayer, including long periods spent in quiet and solitude. Several times (for example Mark 6: 46; Matthew 14:23 and Luke 5:16) we hear how he escaped from the crowds to pray in solitude. The Letter to the Hebrews offers an appropriate summary of the depth, intensity and openness of prayer in Jesus' life: 'In the days of his flesh, Jesus offered up prayers and supplications, with loud cries and tears, to the one who was able to save him from death, and he was heard because of his reverent submission' (Hebrews 5:7). His prayer was answered, but that did not mean being spared the cross. Accepting what lay before him, and united with the Father, Jesus came to peace as he was about to complete his mission (John 17). In this prayer of union with the Father, he asked that we too be one with him and with the Father (John 17:11). That contemplative prayer of unity reveals the loving relationship that Jesus lived in his life.

Jesus' Life of Prayer
As we follow the life of Jesus, we can learn from how he prayed and what he taught about prayer. He is both our model and our teacher. As we have seen, John brings out most clearly Jesus' relationship with the Father, his availability for mission, and his ardent desire to do the Father's will. The place

and importance of prayer in Jesus' life, which is reflected in all the gospels, can be seen especially in Luke, who shows us Jesus praying at all the decisive moments in his mission. A closer look at this gospel in particular will reveal how prayer was at work during all the key moments of Jesus' life.

- It was at prayer after his baptism (Luke 3:21–22) that Jesus received his mission as the beloved Son. That event was an affirmation by the Father and the Spirit of what Jesus was setting out to be and to do. His mission of love unfolded in prayer.
- Before the temptations (Luke 4:1–13), Jesus is described as being 'full of the Holy Spirit' and being 'led by the Spirit'. During the temptations he turned to Scripture and to the Father who was with him. This was a time of testing at the beginning of his mission, a critical moment in choosing the direction he would take.
- Before he called the apostles (Luke 6:12), Jesus spent the night in prayer. Inviting others to help him in his mission was the beginning of a new phase and marked an important decision. It arose out of a time of prolonged and intense prayer, with Abba guiding him.
- Peter's profession of faith (Luke 9:18–21) took place while Jesus was at prayer. At this time, the apostles were being invited to a more personal faith in Jesus and a deeper sharing in his mission. In knowing who he was, they were brought a further step in their relationship with him and their role in his mission.
- Jesus' Transfiguration (Luke 9:28–36) took place during prayer: 'And while he was praying, the appearance of his face changed, and his clothes became dazzling white.' His true identity was revealed more fully to the three who were with him, though they did not understand what was happening. This was a further confirmation of Jesus, the chosen Son who must be heard. The disciples were being strengthened for what lay ahead, which would lead him and them to glory through suffering (cf. Luke 24:26).
- It was following his own prayer that Jesus taught his disciples how to pray: 'He was praying in a certain place, and after he had finished,

one of his disciples said to him, "Lord, teach us to pray"' (Luke 11:1). In his teaching on prayer Jesus tells us to give glory to the Father, as well as to ask in confidence for what we need. We are children of the same Father who sent him. He is the one who teaches us to pray; he is the one who sends us with good news. The Kingdom comes when God's way prevails, when God's presence meets a human response.

- On the eve of his passion, Jesus prayed for his disciples and for those who through them would believe in him (John 17:20). He prayed specifically for Peter – 'I have prayed for you that your own faith may not fail' (Luke 22:32) – who in turn was to strengthen others.
- In Gethsemane (Luke 22:41–46), the prayer of the agony was a prayer at another crossroads, another moment of decision: 'Father, if you are willing, remove this cup from me.' It was a prayer of trust in the one who sent him. Through this prayer he found peace and the strength to continue the journey to the cross. On that journey, he would reach out to others, such as the women of Jerusalem (Luke 23:28).
- At his crucifixion (Luke 23:33–46), Jesus' prayer was one of forgiveness for those who had crucified him, revealing in practice his teaching on forgiveness: 'Father, forgive them; they do not know what they are doing' (Luke 23:34).
- Later, Jesus' dying breath was a prayer of loving surrender to his Father: 'Father, into your hands I commend my spirit' (Luke 23:46). This was the consummation of a life spent in self-giving and self-offering, the ultimate 'yes' to the Father who had sent him. By losing his life he would find it.

Jesus' prayer touched each aspect of his life. His humanity is particularly evident in the accounts of his passion and death. When praying in the garden he wanted the support and companionship of his friends. His sense of being abandoned on the cross led him to cry out in pain to his Father. On the other hand, his prayer of union with the Father was a sustaining and supportive relationship. He turned to the Father in all the situations of his life.

Qualities of Jesus' Prayer

Union with the Father was central to Jesus' prayer, life and mission: 'The Father and I are one' (John 10:30). Contemplative in the midst of much activity, each aspect of Jesus' life was submitted to the Father. John 17 gives explicit testimony to his union with the Father and to his desire for all his followers to share more fully in that same union, 'that they all may be one. As you, Father, are in me and I am in you, may they also be one in us' (John 17:21). His proclamation of the good news and his healing actions were firmly rooted in his loving relationship of union with the Father who sent him and who remained with him. In his prayer in the garden before his death, he was able to surrender his way to that of the Father. He modelled unity and contemplation.

Praise and thanksgiving were important dimensions of Jesus' prayer: 'I thank you, Father, Lord of heaven and earth, because you have hidden these things from the wise and intelligent and revealed them to infants' (Luke 10:21). During his last conversation with the apostles, he prayed, 'Father, the hour has come; glorify your Son so that the Son may glorify you' (John 17:1). He frequently prayed in thanksgiving in anticipation of an event taking place; this was in accordance with Jewish tradition, where such prayer was seen to bring blessing and transformation. As an example, we read how, before feeding the crowd, 'he took the seven loaves, and after giving thanks he broke them' (Mark 8:6). Again, before calling Lazarus from the tomb (John 11:41), Jesus prayed in thanksgiving: 'Father, I thank you for hearing me'. Later, at the Last Supper, 'he took a loaf of bread, and when he had given thanks, he broke it' (Luke 22:19).

The familiar themes we pray about all show up in Jesus' life: praise, gratitude, intercession and forgiveness. Two pivotal moments stand out in Jesus' prayer: the temptations and the agony. The first came at the beginning of his public ministry, and the second near the end of his mission. Both are times of discernment and decision regarding the type of Saviour he was to be. He did not compromise at the temptations (Luke 4:1–13), nor did the prospect of the cross deter him from accepting the Father's will, despite his anxiety and fear (Luke 22:42). The prayer in the garden brought him an inner peace, so that he was able to face his captors with serenity (John 18:1–11). He reached out in compassion to the man who was wounded during his arrest, and healed him (Luke 22:51). On the way to Calvary he ministered to those who were distraught (Luke 23:28–29), and on the cross he consoled the criminal crucified with him (Luke 23:43). Finally, he gave his all in total abandonment to the Father in a final 'yes'. His self-emptying reached its completion on the cross. The unity of will between Jesus and his Father, rooted in their loving relationship, strengthened Jesus in his saving mission.

Jesus' Teaching on Prayer
Jesus gave the Lord's Prayer in response to the apostles' request, 'Lord, teach us to pray' (Luke 11:1). It can be understood as a summary of the whole Gospel and as a model of all prayer. It is a prayer of unity and reconciliation, bringing us into union with the Father and one another. St Augustine said, 'If we pray rightly, and as becomes our wants, we say nothing but what is already contained in the Lord's Prayer. And whoever says in prayer anything which cannot find its place in that Gospel prayer, is praying in a way which, if it be not unlawful, is at least not spiritual' (Letter to Proba, chapter 12, 22). In the Lord's Prayer, we pray both for the Kingdom of love and for what is necessary to welcome it. We ask that God's will be done and Jesus' mission be accomplished. The first part draws our attention to the glory of God, as we pray for the revelation of God and for final redemption. In the second part, we bring our concerns to God, for these are paths that lead us towards God.

The Lord's Prayer reminds us that we are created to give praise, reverence, service and glory to God, and we ask for that gift and what we need to live it out. Jesus' prayer in his Farewell Discourse (John 17) reiterates the great petitions of the Lord's Prayer: concern for the Father's name, passionate zeal for the Kingdom, the accomplishment of the Father's will, the fulfilment of God's plan for salvation, and deliverance from evil.

Jesus spoke of his Father as one who gives good gifts to his children (Luke 11:13), and he told his followers to practise intercessory prayer with confidence: 'Ask and you will receive, so that your joy may be complete' (John 16:24). He promised that if they asked for anything in his name it would be given to them (John 15:16). He himself frequently heard the prayers of those who came to him, as can be seen most clearly in his response to requests for healing (for example Mark 1:40; 5:23; 10:51). In several stories, Jesus praised those who showed faith in this kind of prayer, for example the centurion whose servant was paralysed (Matthew 8:5–13) and the persistent Canaanite woman (Matthew 15:21–28).

Prayer of intercession was part of Jesus' own life. As we have seen, he prayed for Peter to be strengthened and for him in turn to strengthen others (Luke 22:31–32). In his farewell discourse, Jesus prayed for his apostles (John 17:9), while also praying for those to whom they would minister (John 17:20). In the garden, he prayed for strength for himself (Mark 14:36), and on Calvary he prayed for forgiveness for his executioners (Luke 23:34).

On occasion, Jesus tells us what we should request in prayer, for example, labourers to work in the Lord's harvest (Luke 10:2) and forgiveness of our enemies (Luke 6:28). Indeed, forgiveness is a key element in the faith community, as Jesus clearly indicated (Matthew 18:21–35). As well as teaching it, he lived it to the end himself: 'Father, forgive them, for they do not know what they are doing' (Luke 23:34). His teaching and example were to inspire his co-workers to have those same qualities themselves in their prayer and in their lives.

Giving glory to the Father was a key element of Jesus' life and mission, and his relationship with the Father was the source of the peace and joy that his prayer brought to him. Jesus desired us to have that complete joy that he had with the Father (John 15:11), a joy that was found in prayer and lived out in life. He spoke eloquently of the joy of the woman finding the lost coin, of the shepherd bringing back the lost sheep, and of the prodigal father on his son's return, reflecting the joy of heaven over the sinner who repents (Luke 15: 4–32). Jesus also spoke of ways of attaining that joy, ways that are surprising and challenging, as he made clear in the Beatitudes (Matthew 5:1–12). There is a paradox involved in the joy of Jesus' followers, as there was in the joy of

Jesus himself, 'the pioneer and perfecter of our faith, who for the sake of the joy that was set before him endured the cross, disregarding its shame, and has taken his seat at the right hand of the throne of God' (Hebrews 12:2).

Jesus revealed a generous, loving God, who wants what is best for us. Our prayer should be full of faith and trust, since prayer is above all an act of faith, trusting in a loving God who gives the Holy Spirit to those who ask (Luke 11:13). This encourages us to pray with perseverance and persistence, like the friend at night (Luke 11:5–13) or the tireless widow who does not give up (Luke 18:1–8). We are told to 'ask and it will be given to you' (Luke 11:9), but faith-filled prayer goes even further: 'I tell you, whatever you ask for in prayer, believe that you have received it, and it will be yours' (Mark 11:24). Finally, all prayer for Jesus' followers is to come from the heart, and is not to be confused with using many words (Matthew 6:7), for such words can be hollow and without substance (Matthew 7:21).

Our Prayer

Jesus draws us into the loving relationship he had with the Father, promising us the help of the Holy Spirit to bring it about more fully. Jesus' life was Spirit-filled, lived in union with the Father, and his desire is for us to share more fully in that relationship and to live out of it. We look to Jesus, whose life was one of prayer and ministry, as our model and teacher, for his was a discerning life, lived in union with the Father who sent him. Our participation in the life of the Trinity will be revealed in prayer, as happened to Jesus at his baptism. Prayer is to draw us more fully into that contemplative attitude, into Jesus' own joy, and into the union between Jesus, the Father and the Spirit. Jesus' relationship with the Father is central to our call to union with God. Our reception of God's way and our acceptance of God's desires lets the Kingdom break through.

Jesus highlights some aspects of our prayer that are important for us in our following of him, such as forgiveness and intercession. Our prayer should look to the life, example and teaching of Jesus, since his mission is also the one entrusted to us (compare Matthew 9:35 and 10:1). We are called *by* him to be *with* him; we desire to be *like* him and to have his attitude, imitating him by *being sent*; we go out *in union with* him, taking his word and message *to others*. Taking on the mind of Christ is to be missionary, to recognise that we are on a journey, that we are pilgrims in life. It is because we are in relationship with Jesus that we can be sent. Jesus, who was himself sent, sends us in turn (John 17:18; 20:21), so that the will and mission of the Father may be accomplished.

Above all else, we are to see prayer as a relationship with a loving God, in which we are guided into the fullness of our vocation by Jesus, the one who sends us the Spirit who prays in us (Romans 8:26). We desire to be led by the Spirit as Jesus was. Prayer then nourishes our lives and guides us through the decisions, the trials, the joys and the opportunities we face. Like the tax collector, we need to take a humble stance before God, who is faithful and trustworthy (Luke 18:9–14). Our poverty makes us appreciate the generosity of God, whom we are called to praise and thank, since all is gift (1 Corinthians 4:7). God's gift to us, and our reception of it, continues God's saving action. God's gift needs us to have open hands to receive it and a generous heart to share it. Simplicity and childlike trust open us to the revelation of God (Luke 10:21).

Our prayer opens us more fully to God's loving desire, allowing God to work in us and through us as we bring good news and healing to a broken world. Since both tradition and our changing culture influence us, we need freedom to discern where God is guiding us in rapidly changing times. As we live our busy lives, we need time for prayer if we are to be people of life and of hope, guided by the Lord, in our restless world. We live in the world as it is; Jesus did not come to take us out of it, but to send us into it (John 17:15). His prayer was real, in contact with the joys and struggles of life and of the mission given to him. Our prayer must be of that kind, too.

Our prayer in union with Jesus fosters a contemplative attitude, a sense of awe and wonder that renews hope in a suffering world, for it heightens our awareness of the signs of resurrection that are present. God's ways are mysterious and are often different from our ways (Isaiah 55:8). Jesus' prayer and Jesus' way bring inner peace, for they keep us open to mystery, to life and to love in our following of him. Jesus' prayer, when united with our prayer, makes us freer to live in that missionary spirit. Being more available for his mission is a concrete expression of our loving response, as it was for Jesus himself, and prayer and solitude facilitate that transformation in us. Like Christ, we seek the Father's will, and that implies that we desire to carry it out, as he did.

Like Jesus, we too are tempted. It is often when we are most generous that we are most vulnerable, but with God's help we can withstand the temptation as Jesus did (see 2 Corinthians 12:8–9). We sometimes come to a crossroads where we need the Lord's guidance and wisdom to help us to know which direction to take. We need discerning hearts to guide us, hearts that are in tune with the Lord, sensitive to the action of the Spirit and open to the Father's desire for us. This attitude is fostered by prayer, which is a living relationship with the God who loves us and calls us to the fullness of life. This is the attitude that gave Jesus a clear focus in life and an enthusiasm for it, and it is to be the same for us. As discerning people, we recognise that God's mission of salvation continues in our time. God began the good work and is the guarantor of its successful conclusion.

In brief, we are drawn towards a closer union, a deeper 'yes', a more generous response to the call we are given, leading to a fuller surrender in love to the Lord. We are called to union with God and each other, and to guide us we have the example, teaching and prayer of Jesus. We are invited to have a contemplative approach in life, giving praise and thanks to God, turning to God for our needs, forgiving those who offend us, and asking for forgiveness and healing for ourselves too. Forgiveness, reconciliation, trust and abandonment to God are essential elements of the mission of Jesus and of his followers. A fundamental change of heart is needed if we are to let Jesus lead us and have first place in our lives. In imitation of his life of prayer and discernment for mission, we pray to have his clarity, joy, enthusiasm, courage and strength to continue to the end as he did. In this way, we become better companions to those we accompany on the journey.

Reflection

*What does Jesus' approach to prayer say to me
in my everyday life?
How does Jesus' contemplative prayer of union with
the Father speak to me?*

Chapter 7

Spiritual Direction

The Introduction to this book expressed the hope of building foundations for a better understanding of spiritual direction in the human faith story. The invitation is to see God act, and to let God act and lead the way. This chapter reflects more directly on spiritual direction as facilitating and deepening this relationship with the Lord, and looks at the presence and action of the Holy Spirit, leading and drawing us into a loving response.

In our following of Jesus, we are influenced by his prayer and sense of mission. Spiritual direction involves a discerning process, where we seek God's preferred way for us with the help of another. As we seek and follow the way the Lord marks for us, spiritual direction has an important role to play. We will begin by reflecting on how we understand spiritual direction before we look at its dynamics – at how it works in practice. Viewing spiritual direction through the lens of our own experience will be helpful. We may see it as a relationship that sets hearts free, that facilitates the inner and outer journey of life, that helps us discover the deeper reality of our lives, that uncovers the gifts of God, or that brings greater freedom for the loving action of the Holy Spirit. All of these imply growth in freedom, and that growth is important in the director as well as the directee.

Some people do not like the term 'spiritual direction'. Rather than focusing on the term itself, however, we will concentrate on what spiritual direction means and what it implies. In the many different approaches that are taken, there is a general understanding of it as a way of accompanying people on their faith journey – being an *anamchara*, or soul friend, in the Irish expression.

Spiritual direction is understood as dealing with the direction of life, and not just prayer. While acknowledging that there can be wider applications – there can be spiritual direction with groups, for example – the focus here will be on its meaning in an individual setting.

Spiritual direction involves the whole person, the ordinary and the extraordinary, the divine and the human. It is incarnational in the sense that it is a lived reality. There is a general consensus that the real director is the Lord, or the Holy Spirit, though human factors can be influential in how well that is operative.

In the Christian story, there is a long tradition of spiritual direction going back to the Desert Fathers and Mothers of the third century AD. There we find references to individual believers sharing the stirrings of their hearts with a chosen Abba or Amma. In more recent times, these records have been a rich source for the development of our understanding of spiritual direction. Today, this ministry has a higher profile than in previous times, with more people looking for accompaniment and a wider range of people engaged in the ministry. Some definitions can serve to illustrate how it is understood in our time:

- 'It is a continuous process of formation and guidance, in which Christians are led and encouraged in their special vocation, so that by faithful correspondence to the graces of the Holy Spirit they may attain to the particular end of their vocation and to union with God.' (Thomas Merton)
- 'An interpersonal relationship in which one person assists others to reflect on their own experience in the light of who they are called to become in fidelity to the Gospel.' (Katherine Dyckman and L. Patrick Carroll)
- 'Spiritual direction could be defined as a process, carried out in the context of a one-to-one relationship, in which a competent guide helps a fellow Christian to grow in the spiritual life by means of personal encounters that have the directee's spiritual growth as their explicit object.' (Sandra Schneiders)

- 'We define spiritual direction, then, as help given by one believer to another that enables the latter to pay attention to God's personal communication to him or her, to respond to this personally communicating God, to grow in intimacy with this God, and to live out the consequences of the relationship.' (William Barry and William Connolly).
- Margaret Guenther uses the words 'hospitality', 'teacher' and 'midwife' in her definition.

These are descriptive definitions, providing us with a focus for our understanding. They point to the relationships involved: the director, the directee and the Spirit. They suggest a way of reaching the goal, which is to facilitate growth in the Lord, and they invite us to take note of the deeper elements involved. It would be good for the reader to note the particular emphases that are highlighted in these definitions, and the responses they evoke.

All these definitions could benefit from further exploration and clarification of the human person, of the action of God, and of the mystery of that relationship. Ideally, a definition of spiritual direction would include some elaboration of the deeper factors underlying it: for example, the development of the core self as a child of God, and the conversion of heart it calls for, or the freeing of God's gift within. The following definition of the heart in the Catechism of the Catholic Church (n. 2563), which has resonances with the desert tradition's 'stirrings of the heart', is helpful:

> The heart is the dwelling-place where I am, where I live; according to the Semitic or Biblical expression the heart is the place 'to which I withdraw.' The heart is our hidden centre, beyond the grasp of our reason and of others; only the Spirit of God can fathom the human heart and know it fully. The heart is the place of decision, deeper than our psychic drives. It is the place of truth, where we choose life or death. It is the place of encounter, because as image of God we live in relation; it is the place of covenant.

Spiritual direction always takes place in a context. It is essentially about the direction of a person's life in a faith perspective, taking account of the different influences that are present in living out the call. It involves more than freedom for freedom's sake; more specifically, it involves a freedom from and a freedom for.

Before considering other aspects of spiritual direction that are either stated or implied in the definitions above, we will first explore what is meant by 'stirrings of the heart'. This refers to the 'spirits' of spiritual direction, the movements that need direction. In effect, spiritual direction recognises the following two realities:

- We are beings with energy, with eros, with instinctual urges (the 'id' of Freud), with appetites, with desires, with impulses, with inner strivings and with affectivity. There are energies, emotions and movements within us that push us outwards into life and into relationships. The question arises: What helps and what hinders our relationships with God, self and others? In life, we are dynamic, not static. We can be moving in a direction without being aware of the underlying influences pushing us in that direction. We can be driven in a compulsive way or, in contrast, we can be drawn, which suggests an element of freedom. We need to be set free, but what is the direction of our lives? Where there is life, something is happening all the time, whatever quality it has. The presence and influence of the unconscious has to be noted to understand this more fully.

- This energy or movement needs direction. Depending on the direction this energy takes, we are led into healthy or less-healthy ways. Accordingly, to use the traditional language of spiritual writers, we can call these directions either 'ordinate' or 'inordinate' (as in inordinate affection or inordinate attachments). The direction we take will indicate to a large extent the quality of our lives. Growth in freedom to choose a constructive path is an ongoing process and challenge. As we have seen already, viewed from a developmental point of view a child begins life dependent, and is unhappy with any delay to the gratification of its impulses or energies. Over time, the child is faced with the challenge to delay gratification, learning the need to make choices that take other factors into account, including respect for other people. Awareness of that affective energy, ease with it, and the direction it should take are ongoing factors in every life. Selfish tendencies remain as well as altruistic ones, and the freedom to delay gratification or to forego it remains a challenge. The quality of the choices made will say much about a person's maturity.

Movement, direction and freedom were significant for Ignatius Loyola in his teaching on discernment. He noted three influences in our lives: the preternatural, the affective and human reason. In addition to affectivity and reason, he understood that there are 'spirits' at work, both good and bad, that have a significant influence on our lives. From this we can see that we can be influenced from within ourselves, or from outside, or from both together. Affectivity and reason can also influence each other. The daily Examen is designed to help us notice the influence of different spirits, identifying where God is present and active in these influences. It helps us to get in touch with what helps or impedes the loving action of God.

Spiritual Direction as Gift Oriented

Another starting point for understanding spiritual direction is to consider the presence and gift of God, or of the Holy Spirit, that is within each person. This is about recognising the gift of God and setting the gift free, allowing the Spirit to show us the way. Here is a short selection of the many scriptural references to this theme:

- 'God created humankind in his image, in the image of God he created them; male and female he created them.' (Genesis 1:27)
- 'This is the covenant I will make with the house of Israel after those days, says the Lord: I will put my law within them, and I will write it on their hearts, and I will be their God, and they shall be my people.' (Jeremiah 31:33)
- 'Abide in me as I abide in you. Just as the branch cannot bear fruit by itself unless it abides in the vine, neither can you unless you abide

in me.' (John 15:4)
- 'The kingdom of God is among you.' (Luke 17:21) (Some translate 'among you' as 'within you'.)
- 'Likewise, the Spirit helps us in our weakness; for we do not know how to pray as we ought, but that very Spirit intercedes with sighs too deep for words. And God who searches the heart, knows what is the mind of the Spirit, because the Spirit intercedes for the saints according to the will of God.' (Romans 8:26–27)
- 'Do you not know that you are God's temple and that God's Spirit dwells in you? If anyone destroys God's temple, God will destroy that person. For God's temple is holy, and you are that temple.' (1 Corinthians 3:16–17)

These references draw our attention to God's presence and action in our lives, pointing to our God-given dignity. By its very existence, the whole of creation, including ourselves, praises our creative God. As humans, desire for God is inherent in our very being, and by our very existence we are in relationship with God. We are made in the image of God, who dwells in us. God's logo is imprinted on our hearts, as it were, for we belong to God. Our human limitation calls out to divine fullness, and our human emptiness is space for the gift of God to fill. Coming to accept the truth of who we are means recognising our fundamental orientation towards God.

Prayer is already going on in us by virtue of our being God's children. The Holy Spirit is already praying in us. This means that prayer is within us, although it may be beyond our awareness, or partly beyond it. It is a gift to be uncovered, since its presence may be largely unconscious. We are called to bring this prayer to awareness, to make the unconscious conscious. It is what St Augustine means when he speaks of our restless hearts: 'You have made us for yourself, O Lord, and our hearts are restless until they rest in you.' This means allowing the gift to come forth and to flourish. It means giving more freedom for the loving presence and action of the Holy Spirit to form and guide us. It means allowing the gift of God to become more central in guiding our lives in love.

Development of the Gift

There is a hunger in the human heart. Seeking our way home, we are drawn towards God in a life-giving way, but the gift has to be developed. Unwrapping this gift of God, allowing its movement to influence us further, is integral to the spiritual journey. In a busy and noisy world, however, where other interests so often predominate, that gift may be given little space or time for development.

Appreciating the presence of God and our own inner urgings contributes greatly to our understanding of spiritual direction. It reminds us that this ministry is focused on growth, not on problem-solving. It aims at increasing our awareness of the gift of God and the presence of God, growing in appreciation of our own dignity and potential. We have the ability to live the gift more fully, allowing the Spirit more freedom to influence our lives. The call is to incarnate love, just as Jesus did in his coming among us. Our frailty and our need serve to open us to what the Lord offers. We are the earthen vessels that can hold the treasure (2 Corinthians 4:7). The gift is to be lived and shared.

The development of the heart is at the core of our lives as children of God, who desires the fullness of life for us (John 10:10). Allowing God's gift to unfold is important, and spiritual direction is about setting the heart free so that the Spirit can influence and guide our decisions. In light of the above, it is worth noting a few key points:

- Expanding our level of awareness is an ongoing invitation that can be helped by prayer, reflection, spiritual direction, retreats, reading etc. After all, why do we take time to participate in all those 'spiritual' exercises? They provide space for a greater appreciation of the gifts we have received, as well as allowing us to become more aware of unconscious influences and their significance in facilitating, impeding or delaying the process of growth.
- The degree of inner freedom a person has is very significant, and is an important element in acknowledging the gift, accepting it, and allowing it to bear fruit. We can grow in freedom through the

action of the Spirit and through reflective living.
- The level of a person's commitment to making the journey is also important. Is there enough energy and belief present to enable the person to pursue the insight and the invitation given by the Lord? We can grow in our commitment, just as we can allow it to weaken.
- Of great significance is the quality of the choices made. In spiritual direction the focus is on what leads to enhancing the Christ-quality of life. The challenge is to go beyond selfish approaches, to allow further growth of life in Christ, to grow in appreciation of the gifts received and to give further expression to them.

We can learn much from looking at how Jesus accompanied people in their growth in faith and discipleship. His interaction with the Samaritan woman (John 4), the blind man (John 9) and the two disciples on the way to Emmaus (Luke 24:13–35) are instances of Jesus meeting people where they were and leading them to grow in faith and to a deeper relationship with him. Without being asked, these people became missionaries, as they spread the good news that was shared with them. They came to know Jesus (or to know him in a new way), to appreciate the gift he offered, and to share it with others. They were set free from what held them bound, and a new future was opened up for them.

With its stress on relationship and personal encounter, John's Gospel provides a particularly good overview of spiritual direction. Key to it is Jesus' relationship with his Father and his sending by the Father. Jesus wanted to draw his disciples more fully into his relationship with the Father, promising them the help of the Holy Spirit to enable this to happen. In his ministry, he encountered people in ordinary settings, people who were curious about where he lived, or who came to draw water from a well, or who wondered where food could be found to feed the multitude. Jesus then formed a relationship with these people. Beginning from the ordinary, from their concrete concerns, he went in the door that he found open, and brought the engagement to a deeper level – to belief in him, to worshipping in spirit and in truth, to seeing and believing, and even to believing without seeing.

Jesus formed relationships with people who were open to him and his message. He then brought them to a deeper place, guiding them into his relationship with the Father and the Holy Spirit. He opened the gift of God for those people by facilitating their openness to receiving it. That is what we seek to do in accompanying others in their faith. We meet people in their ordinary circumstances, and form a relationship with them to facilitate a deeper relationship with Jesus, the Father and the Spirit.

Spiritual Direction and Counselling: Similarities and Differences
At this point it may be helpful to make a few comments on the differences and similarities between spiritual direction, on the one hand, and counselling or therapy, on the other. Since both set out to help people, it is not unusual for this to be raised. In different ways, they both facilitate a person to grow in freedom, to improve the quality of relationships, to make better decisions and to find direction in life. It is clear that there is some overlap between spiritual direction and counselling.

Sometimes the same person who seeks spiritual direction also asks for counselling, and some of the same elements may figure in both situations. Counselling occasionally involves some spiritual direction, although this is not common, since counselling tends to be secular in orientation, as we have seen. Spiritual direction will generally involve some counselling, however, since issues other than prayer arise in real life. Everybody needs some healing of the past and may need some assistance in dealing with current situations too. In what follows, some distinctions are made for the sake of clarity, although what is presented is clearly limited in scope and doesn't pretend to be comprehensive.

Part of the complexity arises from the fact that there are many kinds of counselling, or therapy. They differ in the attention they pay to the level of regression, the role of free association, the importance of the unconscious, the quality and goal of the relationship, and the kind of interpretation that takes place. Different understandings of the human person and of the desired goals can be implicit in the approaches taken. Allowing for this variety of approaches, the following is an attempt to formulate some general distinctions between spiritual direction and counselling, and to offer some further comments.

- In dealing with human motivation, counselling seeks to uncover the roots of personal difficulties, and tends to have a particular interest in the past and in the unconscious. This is true especially of the analytic types of therapy or counselling. Where it touches on human motivation, spiritual direction also has an interest in the past, but it is more concerned with finding direction and going forward in faith. Compared with the more analytic types of therapy, which foster regression and transference as ways of uncovering the roots of difficulties, the relationship in spiritual direction is more 'real'. While transference arises in spiritual direction, it is not fostered as such.

- Counselling tends to begin with the difficulties that a person encounters in life and in relationships. People usually begin spiritual direction by looking towards the Lord. If problems get in the way of that, then they are addressed. It is like a person wanting to look at the sun, not the clouds. We look at the clouds when they get in the way of the light.

- Counselling tends to deal more with 'human problems', or problems of living, although such situations can also arise and be dealt with in spiritual direction. Spiritual direction, however, is *not about mere problem-solving*, even if there are difficulties in the spiritual or moral spheres to be addressed. Its focus is more *growth-oriented*.

- Counselling deals more with knowing, accepting and changing the self, without necessarily specifying a clear goal for the freedom attained. If it does articulate a goal, it will tend to be more self-oriented or humanistic – for example, to become more fulfilled or to find oneself. The values that are central in spiritual direction come from Christ and the Gospel. Since these give rise to a specific goal – love of God and others – they go more directly beyond the self, and for different reasons.

- God or prayer may not enter explicitly into counselling. Indeed, there are some forms of counselling that expressly exclude any reference to these. Spiritual direction, on the other hand, takes place in a faith context, presupposes prayer and includes God in its horizon.
- Spiritual direction is concerned with discernment, which involves seeking God's will or desire, whereas counselling is oriented more to decision-making.
- There is a human relationship in both spiritual direction and counselling, but a relationship in faith is not the same as a professional relationship. As indicated above, counselling deals more explicitly with what goes on between the counsellor and the one being counselled. In spiritual direction, the main focus is on the interaction between God and the directee, and it involves a three-way relationship between God, directee and director.
- There are times in spiritual direction when consideration needs to be given to referring a person to a counsellor. This can happen when the difficulties presented are too pervasive, or too deep, and require a different skill to help the person become more free in life and in prayer. Since a referral of this kind may be seen as a rejection – or maybe *another* rejection – it is important that this be done delicately, especially if the directee has a poor sense of self. (As regards continuing contact with someone who is referred in this way, there are different opinions among counsellors; some welcome it, others do not. Some counsellors are happy for the person to continue in spiritual direction, but there can be situations where a break from spiritual direction for a time is better.)
- If a directee is seen to need some counselling, it is wise to get some advice as to the form of counselling that might be most appropriate or beneficial for the person concerned.
- While spiritual direction can lead to counselling, when blocks to growth are too deep or too many, the reverse can also happen.

Counselling can flow into spiritual direction when a person wants to direct the new-found freedom towards the Lord. This raises the issue of 'freedom from' and 'freedom for', which are part of both processes.

- It is possible for a person to be in counselling and spiritual direction at the same time, provided it is seen as helpful and agreeable to both 'helpers'.

Given the distinctions between spiritual direction and counselling, it needs to be reiterated that there is also overlap. We can learn about our relationship with God by looking at the parallel with human relationship. We should not be surprised, then, when we react to God in a fashion somewhat similar to the way in which we react to our fellow human beings. The same psychodynamics are at work. For example, if we repress our anger at home, we will tend to do the same when we are angry with God. If we do not trust ourselves or others, are we likely to trust God? It is relevant to point out, however, that God is not limited to that human parallel, since a change in relationship with God can bring about a change in human relationships, just as a change in how we react to humans will be reflected in our relationship with God. It is like two-way traffic, with love of God leading to love of neighbour, and vice versa. As we surrender more to God, we become more open to others also.

It is important to remember that the ministry of spiritual direction is to accompany people, not implement theories. The key question to be kept in mind is: What will help this person at this time? Difficulties in prayer are often rooted in difficulties in life. When a person expresses a difficulty in prayer, it is worth looking at the person's life, since what goes on in prayer can be symptomatic of what is going on in the person's life. Being too busy, for example, while itself not conducive to quiet, can also be a way of avoiding prayer, especially when something difficult has to be faced. It is helpful to recognise that most difficulties tend to arise at the human level, more than at the level of faith.

How well does it work if person is in counselling and receiving spiritual direction at the same time? It depends on the presence of several factors in the spiritual director and the counsellor, for example respect for each other's expertise, the view held of the human person, and the end goals envisaged for the person. If these are not addressed, the spiritual director and counsellor can give messages that are in conflict with each other, and they can even come across as being in competition with each other. There are counsellors who have no place for the spiritual or religion or the healing power of prayer. There are spiritual directors who do not value what counselling has to offer, considering that everything can be done by prayer and the healing power of God.

Some counsellors who respect the spiritual consider that it can be helpful for a person to leave spiritual direction behind temporarily in order to uncover the source of difficulties. That person can then come back to spiritual direction in a more liberated way. In coming to a decision on this matter, it is important once again to begin with the person, not with a theory. It is necessary to focus on what is going to be most helpful for this person, in this situation, with these concerns or issues, in order to move forward in greater freedom. This establishes a reliable criterion by which to evaluate the best path ahead. It presupposes freedom in the spiritual director and the counsellor.

Reflection

What has your experience of spiritual direction done for you?
As a child of the light, are you more afraid of the dark or of the light?
How do you see the contribution counselling can make in facilitating spiritual direction?

Chapter 8

Resistance

Jesus said to them, 'Why are you talking about having no bread? Do you still not perceive or understand? Are your hearts hardened? Do you have eyes, and fail to see? Do you have ears, and fail to hear? And do you not remember? When I broke the five loaves for the five thousand, how many baskets full of broken pieces did you collect?'

They said to him, 'Twelve'. 'And the seven for the four thousand, how many baskets full of broken pieces did you collect?' And they said to him, 'Seven'. Then he said to them, 'Do you not yet understand?' (Mark 8:17–21)

Having reflected on discipleship, prayer and spiritual direction it seems appropriate at this point to look at resistance, since it can show up in each of these three areas or in any combination of them. All of these areas pertain to growth in relationship with the Lord, but in each of them there are possible pitfalls. The Lord's invitation can meet different responses.

While God continues to draw us into a deeper loving relationship, we can be slow in responding to the call. This reluctance or resistance can be seen in the areas of discipleship, prayer and spiritual direction. These areas reveal to us our call and giftedness, but they can also point to our limited responses. What goes on in discipleship and prayer can become evident in spiritual direction. The onward call and the proclamation of ideals do not always meet a ready response. There can be impediments to progress, as we can see in the exchange between Jesus and his disciples at the head of this chapter. There we see how the disciples were slow to understand Jesus and his message. It was alien to their expectations in many ways, and seemed to be pointing in a direction that did not appeal to them. Becoming open to the way of the Lord required changes in themselves, as well as changes in how they related to the Lord and to others. The disciples were being asked to look beyond the immediate to see what the Lord was offering them. He had a deeper message that they were slow to grasp.

Resistance to Discipleship
The Lord calls us and desires to draw us closer. That implies growth, change and development, but there can be resistance to this. Like the disciples, we are human beings who are gifted but flawed. We have potential but we are also limited. We can grow in response to the call, or we can refrain from doing so. That is the reality of our lives. Resistance is a term used in physics, where there is opposition to the passing of a steady electric current through a body or circuit, so that the desired goal is impeded in some way. In our following of the Lord, resistance can be understood as an unconscious process that impedes or avoids some experience or some unacceptable message that is perceived as threatening or too challenging. The change that is required is perceived as being too much at this time. Change requires us to see something or someone differently, be it ourselves, the other, God – or all of these. We need freedom to facilitate the adjustment needed to adapt to some new understanding, information or insight, and to respond or to relate differently.

Resistance is illustrated clearly in the lives of the early followers of Jesus, as they struggled to understand him and to follow his example. On some occasions that resistance was openly voiced, as when Peter opposed Jesus about the suffering he anticipated (Mark 8:31–33). At other times it was implied in their responses, as when Peter, James and John fell asleep in the garden (Mark 14:37). We should note that all resistance to growth in their relationship with the Lord was on the side of the apostles. The same is true for us. God's light shines on us, but we can resist it by putting up the shutters against it, or failing to see it. Our image of God is sometimes part of the difficulty. We may want to accept God on our own terms, and so we resist God's call, fearing it and what it may demand of us. Our ideals can pertain to the Kingdom, but they can sometimes be more centred on proving ourselves, or feeling better about ourselves, and can be an attempt to compensate for a poor self-image.

When we feel uncomfortable or threatened, we tend to defend ourselves in one way or another. New opportunities or challenges can evoke varied responses, from automatic reactions to more responsible and free decisions. Compensation, or escape, can be sought in some form when the invitation seems too much for us. Where resistance is involved, the level of awareness that is present is significant, since there can be awareness of the resistance without an understanding of the real reason that lies behind it. There can be conscious resistance, but more often we are dealing with blindness, not ill will.

The Lord calls us onwards into an ever-deeper relationship of love and service. The ideals that he presents in the Gospel can be clear to us – for example losing our life to find it (Matthew 10:38–39), or selling all to give to the poor (Matthew 19:21) – but we do not have to look far to see how easily resistance and human ambiguity arise, impeding progress. Proclaiming values and principles is different from living them, and ideals may take little account of the limits of life. Yet we can resist the limits and anything that seems to fall short of the ideals. We can resist seeing ourselves as we really are, just as we can resist the message of the Lord about following him more closely.

Frequently, our focus is on the immediate, but the real reason for our resistance can remain outside our awareness. The attraction of the here and now can be stronger than the long-term benefits. We can be more interested in satisfying our emotional needs – feeling secure, affirmed, loved or being in control, for example – than in furthering the Kingdom of God. When the demands on us seem too great, we can come up with reasons for a negative response, claiming, for instance, that a loving and merciful Lord would not expect so much of us. It is clear, then, that our feelings can be very influential in how we deal with change. There can be long-standing patterns of resistance at work in our lives, patterns that can often be protected by strong defences.

The influence of feelings rooted in the past needs to be recognised when considering our image of God and our response to the call. For example, if we have a demanding God, we may resist believing that we are loved and lovable. On the other hand, a comfortable God may make it difficult for us to see ourselves as sinners in need of a Saviour. These factors can likewise affect the quality of our relationship with God and the quality of our prayer, and can be a block in our response to the call. It is possible for us to remain comfortable with what we know, content and secure within that framework, even if it is less than life-giving. Change can be challenging. T. S. Eliot noted: 'Humankind cannot bear very much reality'. We can react to what makes us uncomfortable in different ways, either avoiding it or facing it. We can be skilled at halting progress, and may be unaware of the real reason for it.

Resistance in Prayer
Prayer is an invitation to let go and let God lead, and can give rise to resistance. Prayer implies some openness to change, but blocks can be present in practice. For instance, certain fears can emerge – such as the fear of losing God or losing self, of losing control, of losing security, or the fear of failure or of making an unwanted discovery. Resistance to learning something new can show up in prayer. For example, if we are praying on the call, we will be faced with the consequences of saying 'yes', of asking the Lord to show the way. Letting go of our own way does not come easily. The end result may be desired, but the means may not be accepted. There is often much ambiguity involved: we want and we don't want. We can want to get fit but shy away from doing any exercise! We can want the crown of glory, but not the crown of thorns.

Ambiguities abound. We can subtly seek our own glory, and think we are seeking God's glory. We can do the right thing, but for the wrong reason. We can resist what we are uncomfortable with, certain feelings – such as jealousy, envy or anger – or situations or people where we are not at ease. We may even want to deny their existence, trying to keep them out of our awareness. Even if we do acknowledge these ambiguities, we may resist bringing them to prayer, since we may experience them as inappropriate or not right: 'I shouldn't be feeling this way.'

Resistance can show up in prayer in different ways, for example:
- At the beginning, prayer tends to be easy and appealing, but as time goes on this affective aspect can dry up, and prayer often becomes more difficult, less satisfying. We can find ourselves bored, unable to get into the scriptural text or reluctant to find time for prayer. We may then drop prayer altogether.
- We may stick to a particular way of praying, despite the evidence that change is required. The call may be to come into the desert, but the oasis is more appealing. There can be a harking back to the good feelings we had before in prayer.
- Another sign of resistance is a glossy superficial approach in prayer, where all is love and praise. Our contact with the Lord is not very deep or real; it remains 'nice' and 'out there', rather than being more personal and going deeper. We can resist seeing ourselves as sinners, or being loved by God in a real way. Our own need of God is given little space, and in that way we are able to retain control. In this situation, prayer can be kept on safe ground and there is little launching into the deep (Luke 5:4).
- Resistance can show up when we are faced with something that is challenging: letting go of our own ideas, for example, or being less judgemental of another or entrusting a decision to the Lord. There can be a struggle of wills – the Lord's and mine – and a reluctance to take a risk. (We can sometimes justify this by pointing out that Jesus had his Bethany where he could relax!)

Prayer brings up two aspects primarily: *how God calls us* and *how we are held back, or held bound*. Resistance can show up in both of these. God's call may seem too demanding by asking too much of us, and we fear that we cannot respond; or, in satisfying our own affective needs, we can be dominated by our own issues, enslaved in our own lack of freedom. Defences can be used to deny their existence, or to give reasons why we choose to do nothing about them, or to justify why we gratify them.

Resistance in Spiritual Direction

Spiritual direction is about what goes on in life and in prayer, offering us an opportunity to share and discuss how life has been. It brings up the issue of discipleship and how we live that, with attention to the ongoing call of the Lord. Prayer that is linked with life helps us to retain a focus that is an important aspect of the faith journey, and spiritual direction helps us foster a fuller integration of faith and life.

Of course, what is talked about in the meeting with the spiritual director may not be the real story, or it may be an amended version of it. Our sharing can be selective, and our openness to having our story clarified and allowing the Lord to take the lead may be limited. Resistance can show up in different ways in spiritual direction. Here are some possibilities:

- The directee 'forgets' the meeting, or arrives late. There can be genuine reasons for this, of course, but it is important to be alert to the possibility of resistance when this is a recurring event, or if the directee is struggling at the time.
- The directee 'forgets' what was talked about at the last meeting, or 'loses' the Scripture references given on that occasion.
- The directee resists something that is emerging in the conversation with phrases like 'I don't see it that way', or 'I don't want to talk about it'.
- The directee is unwilling to allow the director to talk about, or objectify, what seems to be emerging from the conversation.
- Even when it is apparent that the Lord is calling a person into further growth, the directee may protest that 'God accepts me as I am' and that the director should do the same. This resistance could deter the director from asking the further question that might illumine the situation and open up the way to change.
- Following on from the last point, it is important to note that the director can be part of the resistance, failing to see or draw attention to what is happening. (This point will be explored more fully in Chapter 13.)

When a person is being held back for some reason, the director's role is to facilitate *freedom from what restricts and what impedes* the loving action of God, so that *a greater freedom for what the Lord is offering* can emerge. The director, in objectifying the experience of the directee, can facilitate that transformation. This entails making the resistance that is present more conscious, thereby facilitating change and growth. It means opening up the gift, allowing its attraction to draw the person onwards.

Facing Reality
Jesus constantly put the reality of discipleship before his apostles. Despite their struggles and failures, he continued to call them onwards. His teaching and his example are important for all of us who desire to follow him, for they give rise to attraction. Nevertheless, ambiguity and resistance will also manifest themselves in some way. Progress does occur, but it is not automatic. In effect, resistance is to be expected and its recognition is to be welcomed, since it then provides an opportunity for growth and change.

The first step is to notice and clarify the pattern, and then to help the directee to see it. Recognition of resistance can come slowly, as in the case of the two disciples on the road to Emmaus (see Luke 24:16, 31). The director must be willing to be patient during this time. It's like waiting in a car at a red light for the signal to change, or allowing seed that has been planted to grow at its own pace. The directee can be helped to pray for the freedom to move forward, and the spiritual director can be supportive by praying for the same gift. While many people tend to see the presence of resistance as a problem, it is in fact a *gift* when the directee recognises it, for it can open the way for the next step.

It is important to remember that conflicting desires are common: 'I want and I don't want'; 'I would like to be more generous, but it costs too much'; 'I would like to be able to swim, but I'm afraid of the water'; 'I want to get fit, but the exercise required is too much'. We have mixed feelings, and we can be ambivalent about growth and change. Growth appeals to us, but the cost can be frightening. Helping the directee to see this ambivalence is part of the process: 'You want to be close to the Lord, but you seem to fear it, or fear its demands.' Unease with closeness to God may be part of a larger pattern in life, including unease with closeness with anyone, including self. In brief, the director should pick up the pattern before looking for the reasons for it, putting content before process. The director needs to be sure that the issue emerges from the directee and is not simply the director's agenda. 'Be alert, but be willing to wait' is good advice.

If resistance is not encountered, if there are no struggles and no growing pains, the question can be asked if anything is happening. The chosen people in Exodus resisted God's way, as did many of the prophets when the role was given to them initially. Jeremiah, for example, protested that he was too young, and Isaiah saw himself as a person of unclean lips. The apostles too struggled with growth in discipleship. When Jesus spoke about suffering, Peter opposed it (Matthew 16:22), and James and John were caught by their ambition for important positions (Mark 10:35–40). It took time for the message to get through to the chosen people, to the prophets and to the apostles. We do not go forward automatically, and self-determination dies slowly.

We all construct ways of dealing with life and with others. We develop patterns that help us deal effectively with life, but we also develop other patterns that resist growth. We develop structures and categories, ways of defending ourselves, that make us feel safe. Being *saved* by God is different from feeling *safe*, and we easily focus on the latter. We can be comfortable on a plateau, feeling secure and comfortable, but that can lead to mediocrity and complacency. The Lord invites us beyond that, to come out into the wilderness (Hosea 2:14) and to leave the mountain of Transfiguration behind (Matthew 17:9). Jesus did not leave people where they were; they were invited onwards by giving up their old patterns. He challenged the faith of the Canaanite woman (Matthew 15:21–28), the response of the rich young man (Matthew 19:16–22) and the good will of James and John (Matthew 20:20–3). Desire and resistance are part and parcel of life, of prayer and of direction.

For the Spiritual Director
It takes time for any relationship to develop and for trust to grow. This applies to the relationship with the Lord as well as the relationship with the director. Likewise, it takes time for patterns in the directee's life to become clear. An initial hypothesis can be formed that needs to be verified. Once the relationship has progressed and a more solid foundation has been laid, there is a better chance for the directee to accept the surprising, to acknowledge resistance, and to be more open to change. In that situation, it is easier for the director to challenge the directee.

In reality, however, the challenge comes from the directee's own desires, life and response. The directee may indicate a particular desire, for example, but in practice may do little or nothing about it. In that situation, the director can draw attention to the desire, or to the resistance, or to both: 'You indicated that you wanted to grow, but it seems you are not able to give much time to facilitate that.' The timing of a challenge is important as well as how it is expressed.

Besides the relationship that has been formed, the director needs enough information before raising a question. This is then done tentatively: 'Have you noticed how you tend to drop prayer at certain times?' Phrases like 'Could it be ...', 'It would seem ...', 'It could appear ...', 'Have you noticed that ...' can help. Pointing out resistance does not mean that the directee will accept it or deal with it. It does offer the possibility, however, that the directee will bring it to prayer and ask for the Lord's guidance. It is important to note that challenging can be done prematurely, and the director should not rush into it, but should rather be willing to wait. An insight is such when the directee sees it!

As spiritual directors, we can resist admitting the blocks and the onward call, both in ourselves and in our directees. We have to admit that unconscious factors, influences outside our awareness, exist and are operative. Admitting them opens us to something new, and what emerges can help growth in discipleship, deepening the response to the call. The more rigid the defensive process is and the more resistance there is to admitting any difficulty, the longer it will take to break through and for any change to begin.

Prayer, reflection, spiritual accompaniment, retreats, reading etc. are all important, but the process of growth tends to be slow and takes time. There are seldom any blinding lights and overnight conversions, such as Saul had on the road to Damascus (Acts 9:3; 22:6; 26:13). We know that God's ways are not our ways, however, so we need to allow for surprises along the way. God's call never ends. The Lord continues to invite us into a more loving relationship and offers the means, but people can struggle with hearing this invitation and responding to it. In accompanying others, we can facilitate growth in freedom and a more loving response to the Lord in praise and service.

Spiritual directors need to attend to themselves and their own growth, including those areas where there may be resistance in their lives. This means being prayerful, reflective persons who receive help for their own life and ministry, including spiritual direction and supervision. All of us have vulnerable points. We have areas where we get held up, and there are times when we feel less comfortable. We are wounded healers accompanying other wounded healers, so it is important for us to be in touch with ourselves – our gifts as well as our frailties – because then we will be better companions for others on the journey.

Reflection

What has been your greatest insight in the past five years? Where are you most likely to be caught?

Chapter 9

Dynamics

Having looked at the call to discipleship and the presence of resistance, we now turn to an understanding of the dynamics, or movements, that take place in life and in spiritual direction. We are aware of desires that lead us to God and of other desires that are not in harmony with these, desires that hold us in slavery to our own selfish interests. St Paul acknowledges that there are conflicting elements within us, different pulls in life that influence us (Romans 7:14ff). Elsewhere, Paul points to something similar when he speaks of the contrast between the works of the flesh and the fruits of the Spirit (Galatians 5:16–26). These contrasting tendencies, whether selfish or altruistic, are part of life and influence the choices we make.

The Oxford Dictionary defines dynamics as 'forces which stimulate development or change within a system or process', or 'a pattern of change or growth, or the forces that produce it'. We all have energy, although particular people, situations, interests or events can increase or decrease its level. While some people are more energetic than others, each one of us has a tendency to move and find a way to direct the energy that is present in us. We have different interests, relationships or commitments in which we invest time and energy, whether people, issues or projects. For example, there are ambitious people who have an insatiable desire for power, control or wealth, just as there are others who show little interest in these areas. Warren Buffet has spent most of his life making money, and now he spends much of his energy getting rid of it! Mother Teresa spent most of her life giving away whatever money she got, making sure it was used for others. In her life of service, she was passionate about giving.

Life is not static; situations change and so do we. An American psychiatrist once said that 'the only stable marriage is a dead one'. The notion of being static does little to inspire life or relationships. 'Tiredness kills' is a sign we sometimes see on our roads. As well as its obvious meaning, it reminds us that people who seem tired and listless, with little energy or initiative, bring little life or vitality with them. Adapting and adjusting is part of life, with internal and external factors both having their influence. As we know from experience, these may also be intertwined.

Life is more than existence. We usually have some goal or focus in life, with plans formulated to attain it and some energy in place to direct us towards it. This is true whether we work from a faith perspective or not. People can be energised by all sorts of interests and causes, including climate change, a greater leadership role for women, and sports of all kinds. For example, we can think of Angela Merkel as a woman of energy and passion who has devoted her life to politics and to a better Europe. Bill Shankly, the former Liverpool manager, is another example of someone with a passion in life. He once said, 'Some people think football is a matter of life and death. I assure you, it's much more serious than that.' Of course, we know that not everything we do gives energy or fosters creativity. Life has its humdrum moments too, when mediocrity and a sense of duty dominate, but a fuller life calls for more than that.

Some Helpful Insights

As noted earlier, there is something within us that moves us outwards, but it needs some control and direction. This is true whether viewed from a psychological or a religious perspective. Both perspectives help us become more aware of patterns in life and their influence. Many different approaches to this issue can be taken, but the choice of a few will be adequate to indicate a trend or pattern. On the psychological side, Freud will be taken as an example. He was a pioneer in this field, leaving a rich legacy to his successors to develop or adapt. On the spiritual side, John of the Cross and Ignatius Loyola stand out as people who had a deep understanding of the human person and of human desires in the interaction with God, especially in the areas of prayer and discernment.

- Freud recognises clearly how the unconscious influences the instinctual energies that are present in each of us. There is a desire – the pleasure principle – to gratify those urges immediately, but by living with others in society some modifying or controlling influences come into play. If we are to live peacefully with others, those urges cannot be given free rein. Living in the real world, the reality principle and the influence of others exert some control over these urges. Words like 'conflict' and 'compromise' come to mind in this approach. While everything remains at the human level, including the reason for controlling those urges, Freud makes a valuable contribution to our understanding, bringing a more developed appreciation of unconscious influences. There is much truth in his theory, even if it does exclude the faith dimension.
- John of the Cross recognises these basic urges, inner strivings or appetites, but looks at them from a perspective different from Freud's, offering a different reason for modifying or redirecting them. Viewed from a faith perspective, John sees how they can disrupt a life of faith and love, and impede the movement towards God, if they are not modified or directed in some way. For John, the goal of life is to see God face to face, although now we only see through a glass darkly (1 Corinthians 13:12). He speaks of three intervening veils that have to be stripped away if we are to come to union with God: the veil of the senses, the veil of the spirit and the veil of death. Stripping away the veil of the senses breaks the pleasure principle, the principle of self-satisfaction, to allow the way of Christ to become the criterion for decisions. We are affective beings, but we need to mortify these appetites since they can cloud our vision. Our inordinate affectivity leads us to what gratifies us now. The more we are selfishly motivated, the less we see because our vision is blurred. For John, appetite or affectivity is key. This provides energy, but it needs to be directed. It can be unruly when

not used well, or it can move us in a constructive way when it is well directed. We need to break the pleasure principle, where our own gratification is to the fore, and be guided by the principles and values of Jesus in the Gospel. This breaking of the selfish motivation is what John terms the 'Dark Night of the Senses'.

- Ignatius of Loyola also begins from a faith perspective, but adds his teaching on discernment. By reflecting on his own experience of inner movements, he was led to consider where they came from, where they were leading, and which ones left enduring peace. He speaks of the urges and appetites we all have in terms of desire and affectivity, and he sees the need for direction in these movements. Otherwise, inner freedom is restricted and inordinate attachments – or disordered affections – become more influential and draw us to selfish living. Ignatius attends in particular to desire, affectivity and inner freedom in responding to the Lord. These are of particular significance for discerning the Lord's way in life, so that energy can be directed away from selfish ends to the service of God. Ignatius gives us a method of discernment that recognises the influences of good and bad spirits, of human affectivity and reasoning, and of the interplay between them. This means acknowledging the ambivalent nature of affectivity, and recognising that we can be misled or deceived. Everything is not as it appears at first sight, as St Paul reminds us: 'Even Satan disguises himself as an angel of light' (2 Corinthians 11:14). We can be pushed in a particular direction, without being aware of the real underlying source. Inner movements and conflicting desires have to be discerned to see what is the genuine good. There is a selfish dimension to life that needs to be curtailed, so that our energies can be redirected to the praise and service of God.

Each of these approaches – that of Freud, John of the Cross and Ignatius Loyola – acknowledges that there is a dynamic quality to life, an energy that pushes us outwards, giving momentum for change or growth. It is dynamic, but it requires good decisions to determine how it is to be directed. Freud's approach is about modifying the pleasure principle when that is required, whereas that of John and Ignatius is about breaking the selfish urge as a criterion of life, and letting Jesus and his way be the guide for decision-making. Both John and Ignatius speak of conversion, of a change of motivation and lifestyle, allowing the Lord to be the focus. Going against selfish desires or impulses is a choice for living with and for the Lord, and is not just a compromise for human reasons.

For John and Ignatius, the issue is more about a change of heart than behavioural change, though this may follow. For them, the energy is to be directed in the way of Christ. This calls for freedom, and involves choice in determining how the energy is directed. The energy that is present in us can be expressed generously or selfishly, depending on many factors in our lives. Awareness and freedom are important, because they influence the choices we make. Conscience is an important factor for John and Ignatius, with conscience seen as coming from within but also from without, from the teaching and values of Jesus. Freud looked more to outside influences, since he did not include the faith dimension. As believers, however, we recognise that God lives in us, and we understand that conscience is formed over time in the journey of faith.

Vision and Values
Our vision of life and the values we hold reveal a lot about us, but they can be distorted and oriented in a selfish fashion. The rich young man wanted to hold on to his many possessions (Mark 10:17–22). The rich fool wanted to build bigger barns to store his crops (Luke 12:16–21). The dishonest manager set about securing his future when he was about to be dismissed (Luke 16:1–9). In contrast to these, Mary was free to say 'yes' to what God wanted of her – to let go of her own plan of life (Luke 1:26–38). Even when our ideals are in line with Gospel values, we should remember that proclaiming them is not the same as living them. Peter's profession of faith at Caesarea Philippi was followed by difficulty in applying it and living it (Mark 8:27–33).

People can be crippled by self-interest, fear or a sense of inadequacy, leaving them less freedom and scope for healthy expressions of energy. If there is lack of movement or lack of growth in life, something significant is being blocked. People can be protective of what they have, or they can retreat to comfort zones, or they can remain on a plateau. Then growth is stifled and becoming is sacrificed. For a reflective person, such an approach is dissatisfying. It is the nature of life to move on; as Newman said, 'Growth is the only evidence of life'. He also said that to live is to change, although change must never be just for change's sake.

We all choose a particular direction, inspired by what we want. Desire is at the heart of life, and has a dynamic quality. Provided it is strong enough, it provides us with energy to move towards some unrealised goal. In this context, we can ask ourselves (or others) useful questions, such as: 'What do you want? What gives you energy? What are you passionate about? What do you do with the energy that you have?' The formulation of goals suggests a direction, and indicates a way in which the energy can be expressed. That energy can be life-giving or selfish, of course, so further questions may be appropriate: 'How do you view life? What is your goal or dream? What means are you using to attain that? Do you detect enough interest and energy that will enable you to move on? What desires lead to movement or action?'

When the momentum or energy is strong enough and is given a direction, or a focus, it moves us with our own uniqueness in that particular direction. Thus, we can identify a momentum that is dynamic and directive in life:

- It is *dynamic*, since it provides energy, enthusiasm, momentum and passion. It touches something significant in us and moves us to respond. It needs some strength, which can be linked with the level of interest, to enable us to move forward.
- It is *directive*, since it leads us to *respond in a particular way*: 'I want to do more to improve the situation of refugees', or 'I want to get out of this challenging situation'.
- It implies *some vision and system of values* that influence the *plan of action* or the *strategy* that is undertaken to try to realise the desire that is present.
- When there are conflicting pulls, it can lead to resistance, but it can also lead to clarity in accepting the cost of moving onwards.

Conflicting pulls can restrict our freedom and influence the choices we make, but this does not have to be permanent. Change is possible.
- It involves a call to make good decisions, in order to facilitate movement towards the desired goal.

Energy has to be directed if it is to be effective. The steam engine created steam that, when directed, made possible the movement of the train.

We have looked at the importance of being dynamic and directive in a faith context. When we take this approach to our ministry of spiritual direction, the vision and values that are meant to lead in a particular direction are clear. We have Gospel-based values centred on the person of Jesus and on discipleship, so we have a specific way and goal for life. To help us grow in our appreciation of what God is offering and where God is inviting, prayer and reflection are of particular importance. Our desires can bring us to God and open us to God's desires for us, so that God's desires may transform our desires. Our energy and desire bring us into a place where God can meet us and surprise us. This means that a prayerful, reflective life is not haphazard or directionless, but one that finds a focus. Our *vision* is formed and clarified further as the journey progresses. We have a view of life and a goal to guide us. *Values* are also to the fore, arising in faith from what the desired goal means. In this way, a *strategy* or plan of action becomes possible. This applies to our own lives as well as the lives of those we accompany.

Vision, values and strategy are part of any life, whether we seek material success and comfort or a deeper relationship with the Lord; they indicate where we invest time and energy. They have a particular significance in a reflective life, where our values do not arise from ourselves, but from the Lord. In this, they form a dynamic process in a life lived with and for the Lord, taking us beyond ourselves. Since there can be conflicting influences, there is usually struggle in formulating the desired goal and moving towards what is ahead. Thus, resistance inevitably arises at some stage. Defences can impede vision and movement in the short or long term. It is in the relationship with God, supported by prayer, spiritual direction and other resources, that we can find clarity. If our desire is weak, or if we experience too much conflict with other desires, we will have too little energy to move on. This is expressed well in the words of Augustine: 'Make me a saint, but not yet!' Desire can be clarified, however, and it can grow; people can change in response to the Lord and with the help of others. In brief, the vision can be clear or distorted, but even when it is authentic there can be resistance to it. Clarification can come over time, as well as the freedom to move on.

Change involves Choice
People do not move on automatically, as we know from our own experience. Our desire may not be strong, and may need to be supported and developed. Our resistance may need to be lowered – whether it arises from self-doubt, or fear or the cost involved – so that a new horizon can be envisaged and more energy generated, with the freedom to direct it. Energy used defensively may need to be set free so that it can be used more constructively: driving a car with one foot on the accelerator and the other on the brake does not work very well, although a lot of energy may be used! Some change is called for when the focus in life is mainly on the self, rather than on others or on the Lord. All of these factors are involved as we accompany others and set out to help them become free to use their gifts and energies in a different way.

While desire can grow and become clearer, it needs to be noted when accompanying another that the desire may not be clear, and that this has implications for the quality of the direction that is taken. The levels of energy can increase or decrease, but these changes do not occur in a vacuum. Before we begin to appreciate the value of physical exercise, it may be necessary for us to do some exercise first! Relationships are significant within this process, since they generate energy and provide outlets. If we are deeply engaged in a relationship, we will have more energy for it and put more time into it, and then it can grow further. Similarly, disengagement can lower all levels of participation. As stated already, passion needs love and love needs passion for direction and depth in life.

Thinking, imagination and affect can influence each other. The extremes of hate and love can serve as an illustration of this. Anger played over in the mind can become more intense; likewise, love can grow in intensity even in the absence of the loved one. Thinking, imagination and affect can influence each other. Love can grow and be expressed more freely; anger can be directed away from a destructive path, to challenge what needs challenging, or bring about change. Thus, our concern is not with the existence of an emotion, but with what is done with it, how it is channelled or directed. Faith life is about directing energy in a constructive way. We look to what brings life, hope and peace to others as well as to ourselves. We believe that we can grow in freedom, and that we can change, reorienting energy more constructively. It is love that brings lasting change.

Reflection

Where do you find energy and where does it lead you? What are you passionate about?

or

It might be helpful to take an example to reflect on as an application of what has been said. Take Saul who became Paul, a complex individual. He was a person full of energy and enthusiasm, which was expressed in action. As a passionate Jew, he knew what he believed and what he wanted to do. He had vision, he was dynamic, and he chose a particular direction to express it based on his values. He also had a plan or strategy to implement it. Following his conversion, the same qualities were evident, but the direction he took was different. His vision had changed, but he did not become wishy-washy, indecisive, unsure of what to do. An account of his life, before and after his conversion, offers us some key points for reflection on the person himself and his mission. One specific text is suggested here: Paul's defence of himself before King Agrippa (Acts 26:9–23). (For this text, see Appendix II, which includes questions that may help your reflection.)

Chapter 10

Dynamic Patterns in Life

The whole dynamic process gives some insights into life itself, and it can be helpful for understanding prayer as part of life. We bring ourselves and our way of functioning with us. In every situation, there is always an earlier story that provides a background and a foundation. As the parable of the sower (Matthew 13:1–9) illustrates, there are different responses to the word of God, and something similar can be said of our lives, too. There are factors within us that influence our choices, whether it is the need to succeed, or to avoid failure, or to be in control, or to keep everything 'nice'. We can be ambitious or passionate about something, just as we can settle for a comfortable mediocrity and have little initiative.

Life presents opportunities for growth. The quality of our reflection, the degree of our freedom and the strength of our desire for growth are significant in determining how we use these opportunities. A picture of how our life is lived can be seen in the quality of the decisions we have made. In that context, it is helpful to note the human factors that can influence freedom, openness and receptivity to the word of the Lord, and also the quality of our response. As Scripture says, 'You will know them by their fruits' (Matthew 7:16).

Human Motivation
Life presents opportunities for growth, but these do not always receive a ready welcome. Each of us has a way of dealing with what we are uncomfortable with, either by facing we it, trying to ignore it, or defending ourselves against it. Key to dealing with the conflicts within us, where we feel pulled

in different directions, is the level of awareness of these conflicts and the freedom to deal with them. We can justify feasting or fasting, spending or saving, being harsh or being soft, being critical or being forgiving, and so on. We need to acknowledge our own ambiguity and have the courage to face it. The following are some examples of areas of potential conflict.

- Achievement can be free, but it can be driven when 'failure' is not a tolerable option.
- Perseverance can be a virtue, but it can be an expression of the inability to give in – stubbornness, in other words.
- Order can serve us well, but if it is too rigid and has to be perfect at all times, it imprisons us.
- Availability is a gift, but it can disguise an underlying inability to say 'no'.
- Being popular can disguise our need to be liked, diminishing our ability to challenge where appropriate.

There is ambiguity and mixed motivation in every life. Everything is not as it seems at first sight. Clarifying ambiguities and growing in freedom are ongoing ventures in seeking the Lord, requiring a discerning approach. Discernment is about sifting through the mixture of human movements to find where God leads, seeking to put order on what may be disordered. Just as swimming is not learned from a book, so we learn discernment by doing it – by reflecting on experience, often with the help of others. In a person who prays, we can expect over time that some movement will take place, some change in life and in relationship with God and others. God does not leave us where we are, but continues to work in us and invites us onwards into transforming union. God was revealed in a new way through the human, and God continues to work through the human.

Clarifying human motivation is an ongoing venture in life. Some general characteristics about personality types and how different people function are outlined in the Enneagram, the Myers-Briggs Type Indicator, psychological personality categories and theories of development. All of these tell us something – whether a person is introvert or extrovert, finds meaning within or without, is more a thinking or feeling type, relies on achievement or is self-sustained, etc. – but each person is an individual, with personal patterns. Labels are not always helpful, especially when they do not readily include the capacity to change. They may tell us more about the *what* than the *why* of what goes on, manifesting patterns of behaviour without indicating the underlying reason for them.

Certain figures from Scripture can help us learn something about how people function and how growth unfolds. In the Old Testament, we read of the faithfulness of Ruth, but we also read about David, who was unfaithful but who nevertheless changed. In the New Testament, the Acts of the Apostles gives us a picture of the disciples that is different from the earlier one we read about. In the gospels, the disciples clearly have a vision of life and declared values, but they are less free to live them, being more concerned with themselves where matters beyond their control are involved. With Pentecost, a change takes place (Acts 2:1–41). The fearful become courageous, those in hiding speak freely, and locked doors are opened, physically and metaphorically. The disciples are less concerned than before about outside threats and their own safety; in fact, they are glad to suffer for Jesus (Acts 5:41). There has been an internal change that is expressed outwardly. People can learn and become freer. Motivation can change.

Patterns in Life
Some conflicts inevitably exist in our lives, since we are human and have not yet arrived at our goal. The Lord has more work to do in us, so there is an ongoing call to conversion and holiness. These conflicts become more obvious over time. The patterns we have developed in dealing with life reveal gifts and prejudices, potential and vulnerability, ease and unease. We all have a past that reveals gifts and weaknesses, openness to change as well as resistance. Our lives can be marked by cooperation or competition, or elements of both. Our past can continue to hold an undue influence over us, often without our being really aware of it. Factors from the past can continue to influence how we live our lives, how we perceive relationships, and how

the future might unfold. In the midst of all else, we like to be in control and everyone seeks meaning and self-worth. In direction, an important question to be asked could be, 'How does this person go about it?'

Patterns are present in every life. In the lives of the apostles, for example, we can note the following:

- Peter was impulsive, ready to speak up, to promise anything and to protest loyalty, but his delivery did not match his words.
- Thomas wanted to know the way, was doubtful and questioning, and sought proof.
- James and John were both ambitious, wanting recognition by being given seats by Jesus' side. The other ten were unhappy, because these two got their request in first. (It is worth noting the irony of the fact that the two who were in fact placed on Jesus' right and left – the thieves crucified with him on Calvary – did not want to be there!)
- Nathanael wondered if anything good could come from Nazareth.
- Judas did not have a good record in keeping the finances straight.

In spiritual direction, it is important to look at human dynamics, noting what is influential in the directee's life. As already mentioned, the person who lives, works and relates in daily life is also the one who prays. For that reason, some similar patterns are to be expected, both in the areas of giftedness and of vulnerability. For example, a person who is predominantly trustful (or fearful) in life will probably find that mirrored in prayer and in the relationship with God. Patterns that are operative within the person can influence, not only prayer itself, but also what is taken to prayer. For instance, undue attention may be given to certain parts of Jesus' life, while others may be ignored. Favourite passages may be chosen at the expense of others that are avoided. A person's interests, desires, fears and prejudices can influence what is chosen or omitted in prayer. Likes and dislikes can influence the choices made.

Real and Ideal

In every life we find the real and the ideal, the actual and the desired. Both of these can be subject to distortion, as can the relationship between them.

This distortion can be manifested in a person's expectations, which can vary from high to low, with many shades in between. How the self is experienced and the expectations that are expressed or implied can be very revealing. Some gap between the actual and ideal is necessary for growth, since it will provide an incentive to move on. If the gap is too wide, however, it will lead to frustration, which can be crippling and lead the person to stop trying.

It is helpful to note how a person tends to function in life and in relationships, as this reveals a great deal. Life is lived between the real and ideal. We aspire to something that we perceive as enhancing life, so that ideals and expectations draw us towards something that is perceived to be better. The energy we have needs direction if it is to succeed in bringing us closer to our goals and ideals. These ideals continue to invite us onwards, bringing with them a challenge that may be difficult to accept, or to accept at a particular time.

All of us have ways of dealing with challenging situations, some of which are constructive and adaptive, and others less so. How we deal with anger and conflict illustrates the case well. 'Fight' and 'flight' are the two extremes, but there are many other possibilities in between; a good indicator can be the trust/fear dichotomy. The patterns present in another can be better understood if the person's background and life story are known, since some of the same patterns can become evident in prayer. They can affect all relationships – with self, with others and with God. It is easy to say with the Psalmist, 'In God I trust; I am not afraid' (Psalm 56:11), but that ideal is not readily reached. It is an ideal, and the reality can be far from it.

Struggle is present in every life. All of us have patterns for dealing with issues, and these include areas of strength and vulnerability. Life is incomplete, so an invitation into greater freedom is always present. New situations can bring to the fore long-standing patterns, often in new ways. Everybody is more vulnerable at some particular stage or area of life, but different responses are possible. Adaptation facilitates moving onwards, whereas maladaptive responses serve to perpetuate the conflict. We can readily apportion blame to others in difficult situations, while failing to take sufficient responsibility for the part we played ourselves. We think that if others changed, all would be well. It may be so in some cases, but very often change has to take place in us as well. We find it easier to point to the problem 'out there' than to acknowledge the contribution that arose from 'in here'. The following diagram may help to clarify some patterns that arise.

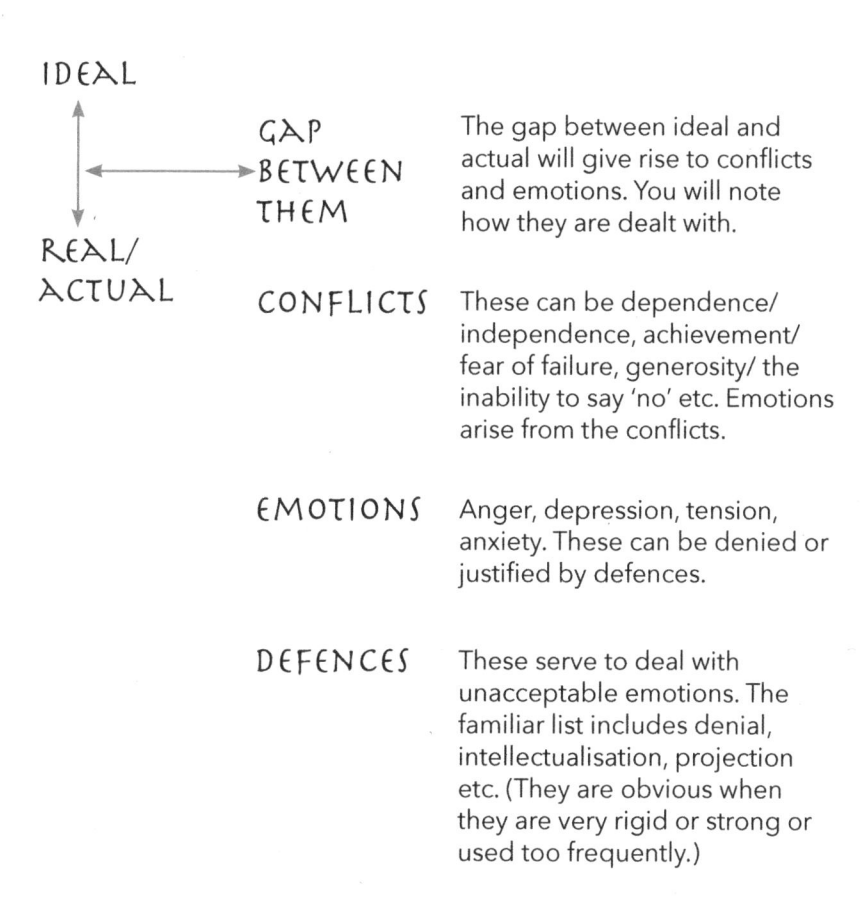

```
IDEAL
  ↑
  |        GAP              The gap between ideal and
  ←——→ BETWEEN              actual will give rise to conflicts
  |       THEM              and emotions. You will note
  ↓                         how they are dealt with.
REAL/
ACTUAL
```

CONFLICTS — These can be dependence/ independence, achievement/ fear of failure, generosity/ the inability to say 'no' etc. Emotions arise from the conflicts.

EMOTIONS — Anger, depression, tension, anxiety. These can be denied or justified by defences.

DEFENCES — These serve to deal with unacceptable emotions. The familiar list includes denial, intellectualisation, projection etc. (They are obvious when they are very rigid or strong or used too frequently.)

It is important to note that the gap between the ideal and the real can stimulate growth, just as conflict can be dealt with in a constructive manner. Emotions can facilitate onward movement. The overall pattern of life will be a good indicator of the quality of integration.

In every life there is one area that is more conflictual than others, even if it is dealt with in an adaptive way. For that reason, it is good for us to ask ourselves, 'Where am I most likely to get caught? Where am I most vulnerable?' We need to remember that a gift can become a liability. Many examples are possible: 'I am generous, but too available, since I do not like to say no'; 'I want to study and do well in my exams, but I want to be with my friends and be accepted by them'. Both of these conflicts can be rooted in the sense of self, thus creating a vicious circle. There can be a conflict between being dependent and being independent, between being generous and being needy, between uncertainty and the need to have the last word. The recognition and the naming of the area of greater conflict can open the way to growing in freedom.

When the director listens to the directee's story over time and reflects on it, some patterns become clearer. Sometimes, it will emerge that the person has a good sense of self and is realistic in life and in relationships. At other times, it may become obvious that a person has a poor sense of self, or that particular conflicts are in evidence. In order to be of help, the director needs to observe how this person tends to deal with these conflicts, whether in a healthy way, or in some other manner – seeking compensation in some form or other, trying to escape from them, giving reasons for them, or using them as justification for avoiding what is challenging.

Life is complex, and people take many different approaches in dealing with these conflicts. When a pattern is perceived in the life of an individual, gifts and limits will emerge, with either one appearing to be more prominent. For each person, however, there is a call to conversion at a deeper level, the level of the underlying attitude that is not life-giving. As already mentioned, the call is to conversion at the roots of the disorder, and not just at the level of symptoms.

Implications for Spiritual Direction
Our ongoing call is to know ourselves, accept ourselves and change ourselves in the light of the Gospel and our relationship with the Lord. Since prayer

and life influence each other, real prayer will touch into the reality of life and will be connected to it. Inner freedom enables us to grow in our image of God and of self, and helps prayer to be more real. If there is a distortion in any of these areas it will become evident in prayer. Exaggerations highlight a pattern, for example when a particular approach to prayer is seen not as *a way*, but as *the only way*; or when significant elements of discipleship never appear in prayer. Everyone seeks a sense of worth and security in life, but much depends on where and how it is sought. It may be in the Lord and in service, or it may be elsewhere – in power, wealth or success in some area. In the earlier stages of life, at least, it tends to be sought outside the self in the approval of significant others.

The life of each person has limits. What is presented in spiritual direction may only be the symptoms of the real issue; the director may have to facilitate something further if there is to be conversion at a deeper level. This will involve helping the person to see what is behind the presenting issue. Anxiety, frustration and stress seek outlets in some form of compensation, for example overeating, drinking to excess or going on shopping sprees. The need to be in control can mask pride, while relying too much on the opinion or approval of others can suggest a lack of self-belief. Recognition of these issues can help prayer move beyond the immediate to a deeper level and the call to change. The aim of spiritual direction is to find meaning in the self as made by God, but this is not readily attained; letting go and allowing God to lead does not happen automatically. We tend to make God in our own image and likeness, reducing God to our own size; in that case there will be little change. Chesterton wrote of the tendency to carve little Christs.

Prayer must be real, coming out of life and flowing back into life. Such was Jesus' prayer. His prayer was linked with his life. There were key moments in his life and mission, times of discernment, when we see him turning to the Father in prayer. Jesus' prayer during the temptations and the agony was real: it took into account his vision, his mission and his current situation, and it was in touch with his human searching and fears. This approach can be identified in the lives of other figures in Scripture

who prayed out of the reality of their situations:
- Hannah, who wanted a child, prayed in the temple (1 Samuel 1:9–18).
- Solomon, aware of his youthfulness on being made king, prayed for wisdom and the gift of discernment to lead the people (1 Kings 3:4–15; Wisdom 9).
- Mordecai and Esther prayed for the liberation of their people in a time of danger (Esther 14).
- Mary in her Magnificat praised God for the goodness shown to her (Luke 1:46–55).
- Zechariah, in his Benedictus, praised God for his faithfulness (Luke 1:67–79).
- In the Nunc Dimittis, Simeon thanked God for seeing the Messiah (Luke 2:29–32).
- In contrast with the approach taken by the Pharisee, the tax collector in the Temple acknowledged his need and prayed for mercy (Luke 18:9–14).
- Paul prayed for growth in Christ (Ephesians 3:14–21).

Life always has some structure that gives us a framework to deal with what arises. These are patterns that are built up in all lives, ways of doing and of being, ways of dealing with issues that we face. We also tend to have patterns in prayer that reflect those we have in life. For our part, it is a matter of assessing which patterns are helpful and which ones are unhelpful.

In spiritual direction, some patterns become more evident in the life of the directee over time. Helpful patterns emerge that enhance life, and these are to be acknowledged and supported. There will be other patterns, however, that restrict life and are not helpful. It is important to be ready to notice these, but time must be allowed for the picture to be clarified before drawing attention to them. An initial hypothesis needs to be substantiated by further evidence. The director must be willing to wait for the directee's awareness and freedom to be increased, so that resistance may be lowered. This applies especially when the person's defences are very strong and over-used. It is good to recall that an insight is an insight when the directee sees it.

Rather than a series of isolated bits and pieces, life is interconnected, and the parts fit into some overall picture. Noticing how they link up is helpful for direction and for conversion at the root level. In spiritual direction, people share their life story, which the director will help them clarify in order to see where the call is at this time. What they go away with is related to what they have shared and their ongoing call. It is the director's role to help them to see what is operative in their lives so that they can reflect and pray on it. Prayer affirms the Lord's way, but it also challenges other patterns of thought and action that may be puppets of disordered affectivity.

Having a better overall picture of the directee's way of functioning allows for different points of entry in raising a particular issue. The director notes the defences, the emotions, the conflicts, the ideals, the expectations etc., before exploring any further. The director's aim is to help, to open the directee more fully to the loving action of the Holy Spirit. Helping the directee to see and understand the gifts possessed and the possible pitfalls opens the way to the next step. God's way is onwards in life and in love.

Reflection

*What do I see as the more predominant
pattern in my own life?
Where am I most likely to get caught with a directee?*

Chapter 11

Dynamics in Prayer

In prayer we presuppose the presence of desire, energy, movement and direction. Desire is an important element in it. Desire is key in our relationship with the Lord, as is reflected in the Spiritual Exercises. Jesus frequently asked people what they wanted, as when he called the first two disciples in the Gospel of John (John 1:38), while on other occasions he responded to requests made to him (for example Matthew 8:1–4). If nothing seems to be happening in prayer, St Ignatius advises the director to question what is going on (Spiritual Exercises, annotation 6). People who pray, or who come for direction, are looking for something: they have some desire to change and grow. A relationship with the Lord is present, and the call is to move from 'What are you looking for?' (John 1:38) to 'Whom are you looking for?' (John 18:4,7; 20:15).

Let's consider for a moment what we do when we pray. We prepare, we set aside a specific time, we get in touch with our desire, we give time to the prayer itself, and afterwards we reflect to notice what has emerged. Later, in the evening, we reflect over the day to get a clearer picture of how the day (including the prayer) turned out, and we look forward to the next day and how we might pray then. It can be said that:

- There is a dynamic in each prayer period. There is preparation, desire, a gift sought, and a concluding friendly conversation (colloquy). After the prayer, there is reflection on the experience. By focusing on what was most significant – where the prayer experience brought peace or turbulence, movement or resistance, where there was affirmation or challenge – an orientation for the next time of prayer emerges. By returning to wherever the most fruit was found, or where there was most struggle, the gift is deepened and there is more freedom to move on. 'Repetition' does not mean that the entire text or the whole scene has to be repeated again. Rather, by returning to what was more significant in the earlier prayer, a dynamic continuation with what went before is established. Some continuity between a particular time of prayer and the next is present.

- There is a dynamic and focus within each day, be it a workday or a day of retreat. Prayer for particular gifts of discipleship for mission are appropriate at the start of the day, while a good way to end is to review the day, to find the overall direction and key elements. By noting the gifts and the struggles that were present, the next day can be faced with direction and hope, and this can have an influence on the approach to prayer for the day. Life is not a series of isolated days. Continuity, change and learning are all involved. Like the chapters of a book, continuity and newness together keep the story alive. One day flows into the next, which provides the seedbed for the following one. This is most evident on retreat or in ongoing spiritual direction. The Examen is an important help in that prayerful, reflective process of reviewing the day in the light of the Lord's love.

- There is a dynamic within a retreat. Desire and direction are present in the prayer and reflection. New material may be introduced in the morning, leading to repetition later in the day, when the main elements that have emerged are given more attention. The day may then progress to a time of quiet prayer, when the fruits of the day are savoured. Finally, the day is drawn together by a period of reflection at the end that provides the way forward for the next day. Continuity is present as each day leads into the next one. At the end of the retreat, the experiences of the previous days are drawn together, giving direction for the ongoing journey.

- In the full Spiritual Exercises, as well as the dynamic present in each day and each week, there is a dynamic at work over the whole thirty days. After a period of settling down and finding a good attitude for what lies ahead, the Principle and Foundation offers a kind of map, reminding the retreatant that our purpose in life is to praise, reverence and serve God, and that inner freedom is the key as we seek God as our goal. Drawn into a realisation of the limited level of freedom present, the retreatant then prays to the loving, forgiving God for conversion, for a change of heart. The realisation of being a loved, redeemed sinner opens the retreatant's heart to respond with generosity, desiring to be part of the Lord's project of bringing good news and healing to a broken world. Wanting to be with Jesus in his mission involves accompanying him on his journeys and being with him in his passion, death and resurrection. By experiencing his resurrection, the retreatant is led to another, broader horizon in the final exercise, the Contemplation to Attain Love. In this contemplation, the retreatant is invited into a greater appreciation of the Lord and what he has done for us and offers us. The horizon is expanded to encompass God present in all things and working in the world. The vision, values and strategies of Jesus influence ours, and we make them more our own as we seek to live them in his Spirit. If we look at the underlying thrust and core vision of the Spiritual Exercises, we are presented with an active God who works as Jesus does (John 5:17), inviting participation in the continuing mission of Jesus. Prayer and call are not for ourselves only; rather, we are called to be sent, and our mission is to proclaim the good news, to bring healing and to be people for others. Prayer is not self-focused, but about relationship and mission.

- There is a dynamic in the Examen, helping us be more in touch with the various influences that affect our everyday lives and to be more open to the loving action of God. We pray for light to see our day in God's way. We are grateful for the gifts received, and reflect on the movements of the day. Following an expression of sorrow for failure to follow the movements towards Christ, we look to the next day with hope, relying on God's goodness. In this way, the Examen provides a direction for the coming day, and can clarify our desire for prayer. The Examen fosters a reflective approach to life, open to wherever the Lord leads us.

Dynamics of the Spiritual Exercises

A great deal has been said about the dynamics of the Spiritual Exercises, and how they involve a person on the path of discipleship. The dynamic is about moving the retreatant towards Christ and the way of Christ, which involves companionship for mission with the poor and humble Christ.

- The Spiritual Exercises offer a path to conversion, leading to a deeper following of Christ. They lead to a growth in freedom to let God's way, which is the end, to be the guide in finding the means to that end. The choice of Christ will be the guide to other individual choices.
- The Spiritual Exercises are dynamic, in the sense that they provide an energy and an enthusiasm that give momentum, touching something deep in the retreatant and evoking the courage to respond to the Lord's call. Desire calls the retreatant onwards, and invites the Lord to transform that desire by bringing it into greater harmony with his own. The Lord knows each one's potential to grow in freedom, and constantly beckons forward.
- The Spiritual Exercises are directive in the sense that they lead the retreatant in a particular way, the way of Christ – the way of being in companionship with him and sharing in his mission.
- The Spiritual Exercises offer a vision for life, providing a system of

values that will guide decisions about living as a companion of the Lord.

The movement of the Exercises touches something deep in the retreatant, brings more alive the gift of God that is already there, and draws the person forward into a more loving response to God's love. The criterion is Jesus himself – his way, his teaching, his example – and his call to engage in mission with him.

The dynamic element is apparent in the lives of all of us, including our prayer lives. It is there in our daily prayer sessions, in days of recollection, in times of retreat and in our ongoing life.

Dynamics of a prayer session:
- There is a time of preparation with the clarification of a desire.
- There is the experience of the prayer time itself.
- There is a time of reflection afterwards to notice what happened and where it is leading.

Dynamics of a retreat day of prayer:
- There is a time of preparation and clarification of a desire.
- There is the prayer experience.
- There is repetition.
- There is quieter prayer at end of the day.
- There is a time of reflection, as above, leading into the following day's prayer.
  (Repetition and quieter prayer serve to deepen what has begun earlier.)

Dynamics of the Spiritual Exercises:
- Principle and Foundation: Dispositions/vision and prayer for freedom.
- First Week: Recognition of lack of freedom in the self and how that gives rise to sin. Prayer on sin in the light of God's love, bringing

a sense of self as a loved, redeemed sinner. Gratitude for God's merciful love, leading to a desire to respond generously, and to be part of the Lord's way.
- Second Week: Call and response. Wanting to be with the Lord in his mission, to be guided by his values, and to make decisions in the light of all that.
- Third Week: Being with him in all aspects of his life including his passion, making us aware of the cost of discipleship.
- Fourth Week: Being with him in his victory, rejoicing with him and in the knowledge that we are called to share his risen life. Contemplation to Attain the Love of God: by appreciating how God is present and active in all things, the whole of life is opened to us as our horizon.

Dynamics of the Examen:
- There is a flow or pattern to the Examen, facilitated by the five steps that are proposed.
- It helps us to notice the movements we have experienced, where they came from and where they lead.
- It is oriented towards freedom and growth; it is discernment in the everyday.

Reflection

Where are you more aware of the activity of the Lord?
What movements have you noticed in yourself?

Chapter 12

Dynamics of Spiritual Direction

Since spiritual direction involves three participants – the Lord, the directee and the director – there are several different relationships to consider. All of the participants are active, so there is a dynamic at work – within the directee and within the director, and in the relationship between them as they respond to the action of God, who draws both of them towards greater freedom and the fullness of life.

Goals of Spiritual Direction
God is active in our lives and in our world, and has a preferred way for each of us. It is the way of love that leads to a fuller life. In spiritual direction we can identify certain goals, such as:
- Knowing the self, which is an ongoing venture.
- Accepting the self, with the gifts and the limits involved.
- Changing the self, which requires freedom. The change involved is not change for its own sake; rather, it is to assimilate Gospel values and the way of Jesus.
- Finding God's preferred way – God's will, God's desire – for the self.
- Putting that will and desire into action.

There is movement in all of these areas over time, just as there is movement between them. There is a dynamic element to these movements which arises from the directee's desire to live more fully with and for the Lord. Change and growth in inner freedom are an integral part of the process. Knowing the self and knowing God serve to deepen the relationship with the Lord, giving greater clarity about how it is to be lived more fully. In spiritual direction, we look for change in that relationship and in prayer.

In spiritual direction, the directee comes with some desire that may need to be clarified. There is the energy that prompts a person to embark on this journey, and this energy can grow and can create more energy. By a prayerful and reflective life, a person is sensitised to the movements of the Spirit, so that direction is at least implicit, though it is frequently explicit, too. This direction comes from the invitation and guidance of the Lord, and not from the spiritual director, so that the more a directee is in touch with the promptings of the Spirit, the less the spiritual director has to do. In that case, it may mean no more than confirming or affirming the movement that is emerging. As the directee is drawn by the Lord into a deeper relationship and towards transforming union, desires are clarified and transformed.

In accompanying others, we need to be sensitive to the work of the Spirit, while also being aware of patterns in life that facilitate or impede movement. This is true of the director as well as of the directee, since the director can get in the way of movement. Given that there are two human beings involved, the gifts and limitations of each need to be kept in mind. There is much potential for good in their interaction, but there are possible pitfalls too. Self-knowledge is important in the spiritual director, so that the focus of the exchange is on the call and response of the directee.

The dynamics within the spiritual director have to be kept in mind, as well as the relationship with the directee. The freedom of the spiritual director to listen, to stay with the directee, to give the directee freedom to make a personal journey in the Lord is of huge importance. It is good to recall what John of the Cross said about obstacles to growth in the spiritual life: they can come from the devil, from oneself or from the spiritual director! The spiritual director can facilitate movement but can also get in its way. So, while the focus here may be primarily on movement in the directee, it is important to keep an eye on the spiritual director in the relationship, to ensure that the way of the Lord remains central in their exchanges.

A Model of Spiritual Direction

There are different approaches to spiritual direction, just as there are different settings in which it is carried out. It is an adult-to-adult relationship involving regular meetings. It is advisable for the directee to come to the meeting prepared, having spent some time reflecting on the time since the last meeting. Spiritual direction can be perceived as a religious experience, since it takes note of the presence of God in life and how that influences the choices made and the direction taken.

A simple model for a directee who comes, let us say, monthly, might look something like this:

Experience
The directee has the experience of life over the past month, including prayer experience and how it relates to life.

Reflection on the experience
Before coming to the spiritual director, the directee reflects on this experience, noting what is of greater significance in it. This helps the directee to clarify what is to be shared in the meeting.

Sharing
The directee shares this reflected experience in the meeting with the spiritual director.

Clarification
Dialogue, and possibly discernment, takes place about what is shared. It involves noting what emerges from the conversation about the experience of the past month.

Onward direction
In the light of the clarification, what is the call, the desire, the draw now experienced? The more significant moments in the

meeting provide the basis for the next step, by suggesting the way forward. As well as direction in prayer, some practical steps may be included here, for example a decision to become reconciled with another. What emerges leads back into life, providing the starting point for the next phase of the faith journey and for the next spiritual direction meeting. What the person will take to prayer arises from this conversation.

We might recall the Emmaus story here once again (Luke 24:13–35), since it can serve as an illustration of this model.

- The painful experience of the passion and death of Jesus a few days previously was uppermost in the mind of the two disciples.
- Their reflection on the events left them disillusioned, their hopes dashed, as is evident from their sharing.
- They shared their story with the stranger who had joined them, acknowledging how it affected them and how they did not believe the reports of the women.
- Jesus clarified the situation for them, helping them to reinterpret their experience and revealing to them the true meaning of the prophets and the events that had taken place.
- Jesus then waited for the two disciples to invite him to stay with them.
- Recognition of Jesus at table led them to further reflection on the whole journey, bringing further clarity. At this point, they did not have to be told the direction to take: it was obvious. They set out on another journey immediately, this time with a very different disposition.

In brief, we can say that Jesus models spiritual direction for us. He listened, formed a relationship, clarified, waited for an invitation, and opened the way for further revelation, indicating the way forward.

Spiritual Direction is a Discerning Process
The director has to allow time for the profile of the directee, with its influential patterns, to become clear. Over time, however, as the director listens to the story of the directee, the profile and patterns become more evident. Noticing the movements that are present, and their direction, helps to bring greater clarity to the gifts and generous responses of the directee, just as it helps to clarify the challenges and issues that can slow up progress in the Lord.

In accompanying people, we set out to help them appreciate and develop their gifts, as well as assisting them to become more liberated from the things that restrict them. Our starting point is a conviction that people can change, motivation can be clarified, new desires can arise, and a different direction can be chosen and followed. We acknowledge that there are gifts in each person, just as there are challenges and conflicts in all of us as limited human beings. There is always a call to conversion, then – conversion at a deep level, reaching down to the roots of those patterns that are not life-giving. The invitation is to go beyond the surface level, to the underlying influence or attitude.

In reflecting on the life and experience of the directee, it is helpful to keep images of God and of the self in mind, as well as the relationship between them. These two images and prayer are interconnected and they influence each other in a dynamic relationship. We may recall once again the story of the Pharisee and the tax collector in the Temple (Luke 18:9–14), how each of them saw God and the self, and how the Pharisee saw the tax collector. These perceptions influenced their prayer. God may be experienced as a judge or bookkeeper, and the sense of self may vary from very inflated to very deflated. Images of God and of self can change, as can prayer. The Lord finds us where we are, but does not leave us there.

We know that God is active in our lives, and that not everything is our own doing: 'No one can come to me unless drawn by the Father who sent me' (John 6:44). We do not speak of a remote, uninterested God, but of a God who is close, who desires that we have life and have it to the full (John 10:10). We live in relationship with God, with others and with all God's creation. Good relationships provide a momentum for growth, for they are dynamic in the best sense. They give more energy, pointing out a direction that is in tune with the values of the Gospel.

When we are in love, we want to be with the one we love. We become freer and grow in understanding, although change in the other will challenge us to change, sustain and support the relationship in a healthy way. The notion of a static relationship does not inspire. God is not static in relationship with us, but desires us to be drawn into transforming union. In a prayerful life, facilitated by spiritual direction, the movement is into Christ, into a deeper love, into discipleship, into companionship for mission and service. Opting for Jesus and his way is foundational, and guides other choices that we make.

Given the various influences that we experience in human life, as well the unconscious factors, the need for discernment in our own lives and in the lives of others becomes clear. It is a dynamic process. We acknowledge that God has a preferred way that can be known, and as spiritual directors we set out to help another to find it. The desire is for a deeper love, for truth and for freedom, as this is where enduring peace will be found. We can grow in relationship with the Lord and we look to what facilitates that growth. The word of God is alive and active, continuing to invite us forward into a fuller life (Hebrews 4:12).

Reflection

What movement do you note in prayer and in life?
Where are the wellsprings that nourish and refresh?

Chapter 13

Dynamics of the Spiritual Director

The gifts and the limitations of the spiritual director play a significant role in this ministry and in the relationship. The fact that there are two human beings involved means that there are gifts and pitfalls at play for each of them and for the relationship. Every spiritual director brings skills to the ministry but has areas of vulnerability, too. The spiritual director can facilitate or get in the way of the action of the Spirit.

The spiritual director is in a privileged position in the important ministry of accompanying others on their faith journey. How well the spiritual director functions, internally and externally, matters greatly. It is presupposed that the director, on taking on the role, is adequately trained, is competent, and has regular updating and sufficient support. A list of the skills that are desirable, and the degree of self-knowledge and freedom that would be helpful in utilising them, would occupy a lot of space, but a few important qualities are highlighted here.

A spiritual director has to be a person of prayer and faith, seeking to grow in relationship with the Lord. The spiritual director needs freedom in facilitating this growth in the directee, and some growth is expected in both the director and the directee. Change can occur in each of them as well as in their interaction, unless there are blocks that impede this. Having spiritual direction themselves is an important support for those who accompany others as they seek to grow in the Lord.

Respect for and appreciation of the dignity and uniqueness of each person is important in this ministry, as well as the ability to listen. The director needs the skill and the freedom to help *this individual* in *this unique situation*. This implies that *this spiritual director* may not necessarily be the right person *for this individual*. Each person is a gift of God, destined for the fullness of life and love with God. God's story meets the human story, bringing a message of freedom, hope and joy. It means being open to the surprising ways of God.

Spiritual direction is a ministry of service to the faith community, in which those called respond to the Lord by being available to others. It is a ministry in which the spiritual director continues to learn over time and with experience. Lives, prayer and relationships change, as do the level of interaction and the quality of communication. Knowing the self and getting to know the directee more fully are ongoing invitations in the relationship, as neither one is static.

Qualities such as openness, flexibility, compassion and trust are important, as is generosity with time and talent. Spiritual direction is a ministry that has the directee's best interests at heart, so it is important to know what the ministry entails, as well as one's own gifts and limitations in it. Updating in spirituality, theology and skills is integral to this. Supervision is a normal part of the ministry, helping the director with self-care, as well as renewing accountability in following pastoral guidelines and an appropriate code of practice. The spiritual director is in a privileged position of influence, needing careful monitoring and self-discipline.

Relationship with the Directee
It must be remembered that spiritual direction is a specialised relationship, the goal of which is to help the directee to respond to the call of the Lord. It is important to clarify from the outset what spiritual direction means and the different roles involved. It is a relationship in which both the director and directee bring their gifts and vulnerabilities to the encounter. At the beginning, it is important to give time to forming a good working relationship where trust can develop. This will facilitate the onward journey, when the primary focus is on the Lord.

It is important for the director to be open to the Lord's surprising ways.

The director needs to recognise the sacred interaction between the Lord and the directee and have reverence for it. This means that the gifts present should be acknowledged and a generous response affirmed, while attention is also paid to the invitation to a fuller life in love. As trust develops, new aspects of the Lord's relationship and call come into prominence, and it is easier at that point to draw attention to areas where the directee is less free, or where signs of resistance may be appearing

As regards the meeting between the spiritual director and the directee, it is important to remember that God is the third person in the relationship. The director can be significant for the directee, for good or for ill, but the relationship with the Lord is *prior to* and *independent of* the relationship with the spiritual director, who does not create that relationship, but is there to facilitate and foster it. The spiritual director's role is to facilitate growth in freedom and generosity in the directee, in response to the Lord. The focus is on the relationship of the directee with the Lord, and how real that relationship is. Confirming what is good in the other, the director helps the directee to discern where the Lord is leading, often noting the challenge or the invitation that this entails. It should be noted, however, that the *spiritual director does not discern for the directee*, but is there to help the directee to discern the Lord's call.

It has to be acknowledged that the spiritual director can impede growth, and it is to this aspect that we will now turn our attention. John of the Cross gives a lot of space to this in his teaching on spiritual direction, aware that the spiritual director can get in the way of the loving action of God. What goes on between the two human persons can help in the journey of life, but it can also get in the way of the action of the Holy Spirit, and even impede it. In what follows, the intention is not to deny the giftedness of many spiritual directors, which is greatly to be cherished. Such people do not create difficulty or impede movement.

The relationship of director and directee is not a haphazard one, since it has presuppositions, goals and a context. It is not a relationship of friendship, since the focus is on the directee's relationship with the Lord. God has a plan

– a preferred way, a desire, or a dream – for this person. The director can help the directee respond to God's plan by creating an easy working relationship that is conducive to trust, so that the Lord's ways can be revealed. The Lord's plan covers all aspects of a person's life, but the directee's prayer can be expected to provide a focus. This implies that prayer is linked with life and flows back into life.

Many of the difficulties that arise in spiritual accompaniment come from the human interaction, from the dynamics involved in the relationship. For that reason, directors must know their own needs and feelings, to ensure that these do not predominate without their awareness. Unacknowledged expectations on the part of directors can have an undue influence. For example, an expectation that every meeting must end on a happy note, with everything resolved – 'I do not like anyone leaving me unhappy' – may be saying more about the spiritual director than the directee. Another problem can arise from directors' 'shoulds', since these can colour the whole relationship and the process of direction. When problems arise, directors can sometimes put it outside themselves, refusing to admit their own needs: 'It is the fault of this stingy non-cooperative directee.' Spiritual directors can sometimes deny painful feelings in themselves – 'I am never angry'), or adopt a superior attitude ('Thank God that I am not like the rest of humankind'). Spiritual directors who have an awareness of what is going on in themselves can focus more clearly on the directee, and be more objective about what *the real agenda* is.

The issues that are important to spiritual directors themselves – comfort with self, a preferred way of praying, concern for justice, relationships with authority figures – can influence the interaction with the directee. Feelings from other relationships can be brought into spiritual direction, often unawares, and these may have an undue influence on the relationship. As a result, the relationship can end up being very comfortable or very confrontational, or it can lead to collusion. In all these situations, the Lord becomes secondary, and what is of lasting value can be missed. The human interaction can play too dominant a role to the detriment of what is meant to be happening.

The difficulties that arise in the spiritual direction relationship tend to come from the two people involved, rather than the Lord. The Lord invites people onwards, and there may be challenges in this and resistance to them, since there is a cost to discipleship. Where two people are involved, however, each with different needs and backgrounds, a lot can happen at the human level. Difficulties can arise from either one of them, or from both, which can interfere with the process of spiritual direction. The human interaction can take on too much significance, leading to the focus becoming blurred, so that the action of the Spirit is not given its due place.

Over a period of time, directors get an idea of how a directee functions. If they sense that nothing is happening, or if they find themselves bored, or end up hearing the same story over and over, or feel they are not meeting the real person, then there is good reason to explore further what is going on. Lack of movement is to be noted, and needs to be explored, since it may suggest resistance on the part of the directee to something that is emerging. Spiritual directors need to be alert to this, so that they do not become part of the resistance or fail to help the directee to get in touch with it.

It may be helpful at this stage to look at some areas where focus can be lost in spiritual direction, and where human factors can get in the way of growth in the Lord.

Possible Difficulties for the Spiritual Director

Difficulties can arise in many ways in the spiritual direction relationship, and different categories can be identified, such as the breaking of appropriate boundaries, the absence of a 'professional' approach in the interaction, the undue influence of the director's needs and feelings, or the director's lack of skill in accompanying the other. It is always important to remember that spiritual direction is not a social relationship, or a way of finding friends, or a way of fulfilling one's selfish desires. It is a ministry of service.

The following are some practical guidelines in managing the relationship between the director and the directee, including areas where conflicts can arise and direction can be lost.

- *Meetings require privacy.* Interruptions, whether a knock at the door or a telephone ringing, interfere with the process. This is basic, but it needs to be stated as a preliminary requirement.
- *Boundaries are to be respected.* It is clear that boundary violations are contrary to the sacred nature of the relationship. Any enticement to violate boundaries, or any expression that compromises the relationship, must be viewed as belonging to this category. As a special type of relationship, spiritual direction needs clear boundaries to facilitate the loving action of God. The spiritual director is never to get in the way of that. Other relationships with a directee may sometimes be present – for example, common membership of a Church group – but these should not be in conflict with, or compromise in any way, the spiritual accompaniment relationship.
- *Confidentiality is a basic requirement.* What goes on between the director and directee is sacred, and is not to be shared elsewhere. Nevertheless, confidentiality is not absolute. In exceptional circumstances, such as a threat of self-harm or harm to another, or where child safeguarding is involved, confidentiality does not hold. This is true especially if children are at risk, when the civil authorities are to be informed. (In this regard, it is important for directors to check the legislation where they live and minister.) Apart from these exceptional circumstances, any breach of confidentiality is a serious matter.
- *False expectations of the relationship need clarification.* The directee's perception of spiritual direction itself, or of the director's part in it, may be quite different from the director's understanding of it. There can be distorted images and false expectations of the meetings, and these may be linked with unclear roles. For this reason, expectations should be checked at the beginning of the relationship. Where the spiritual direction relationship is not clarified, the directee may view the director as a problem-solver or 'rescuer' in a time of suffering, or may see the director as an authority figure who will give

the definitive judgement about how to pray, for example.
- *Colluding is to be avoided.* Faced with an experience or interpretation that the director is uncomfortable with – for example a conflictual relationship – collusion on the part of the director is a danger. This could lead to the director condoning something, or giving 'plausible' reasons for it: 'God would not ask anyone to do that.'
- *Confusing acceptance and approval is to be avoided.* The director listens, accepts and understands, but that does not mean that the director agrees with or approves of all that has been shared.
- *Unclear communication needs to be eliminated.* Does the director understand the directee and does the directee understand the director? It is important for the director not to presuppose the meaning of some of the directee's words or phrases, such as 'Life is a mess', 'Prayer was terrible' or 'Nothing happened in prayer'.
- *Patterns of human behaviour need to be understood.* This takes more than common sense, although that does help. Examples: a lack of prayer may be due to a directee's fear of being alone; or a person may be more at ease with understanding than with the emotional aspects of the self.
- *Concluding the story before it is told is to be avoided* – for example, interrupting a directee's story, finishing sentences or interpreting prematurely.
- *Eagerness to share one's own experience should be curbed.* Talking about one's own experience can mean that not enough space is given for the directee's narration.
- *Giving advice according to one's own ideas is not helpful* – 'I'm telling you what to do', or 'I suggest' are examples of this.
- *Leading rather than following is to be avoided.* Being over-directive can lead to interpreting too much, or asking too many questions. If this occurs, it is good for the director to ask why this is happening. It could stem from anxiety or a need to feel useful.
- *Playing God is not wise.* This can take the form of 'I know what is

good for you, but you aren't ready for it yet.' If a God complex is present, what does it say about the director?
- *Steering the directee away from certain feelings is to be avoided.* Sometimes a director is uncomfortable with certain feelings, such as anger or love, and can prevent the directee from getting to them or expressing them. Such defensive or anxious reactions can arise especially if these feelings are directed at the director. The director may fail to give adequate space for these feelings to be explored, and the real issue can be missed.
- *Attributing the director's own feelings to the directee is bad practice.* If that happens, the question needs to be asked: Who is getting angry? Who is uncomfortable?
- *Losing respect for the directee is a danger to be avoided.* The director may come to see the directee as lazy, stupid, weak, un-cooperative or in some other negative way. In that case, the director is more likely to 'forget' appointments.
- *Unwarranted reassurance is not helpful* for the directee – 'I wouldn't worry about that if I were you' is an example of this.
- *Instinctive sympathies in the director need to be watched.* A director may have instinctive sympathy for the 'underdog', for example, and be inclined to take sides with a 'victim': 'I know what it's like ... my superior (or my minister, my husband, my wife, my bishop) is like that.' This can mean collusion.
- *The danger of holding a directee back should be noted.* This can happen because of guilt on the director's part – for example, if the directee is expressing a desire for more prayer than the director practices, or seems to be enjoying greater freedom than the director.
- *The director needs to avoid getting too involved.* Over-identifying with or taking too much responsibility for the directee needs to be spotted. There can be various reasons for this. The director may be personally attracted to the directee, for instance, or too much pity may be evoked. If something arises that could make the relationship

more difficult, the director may be unwilling to face it, perhaps fearing to lose the directee. In these situations, the director's own conflicts are to the fore.

- *The director should watch the need to be successful.* This can manifest itself in statements like 'All my directees are into mystical prayer.' It can lead the director to be impatient and to promote a particular way of praying.
- *The need to be liked or accepted is to be avoided.* This can manifest itself when the director is too passive and gives too little direction. The fear of losing a directee can result in an absence of challenge.
- *Failure to recognise the individuality of the directee can cause problems.* There is always the danger of putting a person into a box. Nobody is a number that fits neatly into a category. Each person has an individual relationship with the Lord.
- *The director should avoid the need to end every meeting nicely.* The directee does not have to go away happy each time. The director's need in this case may cheat the directee of some 'growing pains'.
- *Holding on to a directee too long is to be avoided.* If it becomes clear that it would be better for someone else to accompany this person, then it is time to let go.

Attention needs to be given to anything that could compromise the relationship or give mixed messages. It is helpful to remember that no two situations are identical. For instance, it may be appropriate to be more supportive of one directee than another, or to be more supportive of a directee in one situation than in another. Respect for individuality and recognition of individual stories is essential. Retaining a 'professional distance' does not mean that the director cannot reassure or affirm on occasion. If there is too much of it, however, something else is at work.

Mentioning the possible difficulties in the spiritual direction relationship, as listed above, is not to ignore the gifts that facilitate the ministry of spiritual direction. The qualities that make for good relationships are to be noted and valued, qualities such as love, faith, compassion, openness, good listening, the ability to remember, the showing of respect and the freedom to raise issues. These can help the director understand the other person and how the Lord may be at work. The director needs to be open to the many ways in which God works. A good question for the director to ask is, 'Where was I surprised?'

Directees can inspire us with their level of commitment, their generosity with time and service, and their faithfulness to the Lord, often in difficult situations. We learn from those we walk with. This is a ministry where more is received than is given. In a ministry that is growth-orientated, we recognise the gifts of others and allow space for development, thereby enabling the interaction to be life-giving.

Reflecting on Experience
It is important for directors to reflect on their experience, since it fosters learning and facilitates growth. Spiritual directors are human and they themselves have many of the tendencies outlined above, although these are not all equally prominent in everyone. Depending on situations, different aspects of the director's life are called forth in the interaction. These tendencies exist and are present in every life; what the director does with them is what is truly important. The director's awareness of these, the ability to notice what goes on and the freedom to make good decisions can ensure that the Lord will have the primary place. Good pastoral ministry allows the Lord to be the focus, and at times that means the director keeping out of the way. While the role of spiritual director is important, we need to remember that we are wounded healers: 'We are worthless slaves; we have done only what we ought to have done!' (Luke 17:10).

Recognition by directors of the gifts and limitations they possess can facilitate the accompaniment of others, as well as ensuring that good practice is followed in this ministry. Accompanying others does not require that directors have it all resolved, but it does demand that they be honest with the themselves, with the directee and with the Lord. Directors' awareness of their own issues can help to keep these out of the meeting. Directors can then have some control of these issues, and can direct them in a constructive way. Directors need the freedom to ask what is relevant and helpful for understanding a directee and for facilitating further growth. A helpful question to keep in mind is: 'What do I need to know to be of more help to this person now?'

Change and growth take place in the director who accompanies another. There is a call to further freedom and greater openness to the Lord's surprising actions. The director learns from directees and cannot fail to be inspired by their generosity, their honesty in times of failure, their faith, and their fidelity in times of struggle. These are people who are searching and who desire to do better, and who trust the director to facilitate that. That is a humbling experience for the director. God's way continues to be onwards.

Reflection

How have I been changed by those who come to me for spiritual direction?
What will facilitate my ongoing growth in the ministry?

Chapter 14

The Onward Journey

In the Introduction we saw how the story of the two disciples on the way from Jerusalem to Emmaus involved an external and an internal journey. Walking with Jesus brought the two travellers further self-knowledge, and they came to know Jesus in a new way, bringing the relationship to a new place. The journey brought insight and freedom, enabling the disciples to make the reverse journey from Emmaus to Jerusalem in a very different frame of mind. As a result of their experience, they were changed. The word of God is a living word, and it continues to speak to us in the reality of our lives and of our time. Like the two disciples we too have made a journey through these reflections, entering into a fuller understanding of what goes on for us as people of faith, and what facilitates the quality of the decisions we are called to make. To close these pages, and to draw together what has been presented here, it may now be appropriate to reflect on another Scripture story: the parable of the Prodigal Son (Luke 15:11–32).

The Story of the Prodigal
Like the Emmaus story, the parable of the Prodigal involves two journeys – going away and coming back – but the reasons are different in each. At first sight, it is a human story of alienation and reconciliation, but in fact there is more, and a deeper meaning emerges as the story unfolds. It begins with the selfish desires of the younger son as he cries out for immediate satisfaction. He wants freedom to go away, to be in control of his own life, and to have resources at his disposal to gratify himself. By being given his share of the

property that was to come to him, he is given this opportunity. The external journey that then takes place is driven by what is internal, by his desire to be in control of his own life, to decide for himself, to gratify himself. There are elements of internal and external slavery in this story, ending with a liberation that opens him up to something further.

Having arrived in the distant country, the Prodigal squanders his property in dissolute living (Luke 15:13). In Freudian terms, he is living by the pleasure principle, satisfying his immediate urges; in the language of John of the Cross, he is dominated by his appetites, by his inordinate affectivity; for Ignatius, he has inordinate attachments, so that the end he arrives at reveals the inadequacy of the means taken. In his self-centred life, focused on satisfying his immediate wants, the Prodigal is a slave to his own satisfaction.

He is brought down to earth when all his resources are gone. His fair-weather friends disappear, and he has to settle for work that is abhorrent to anyone of his people – feeding pigs. This experience causes him to reflect, to recognise his situation, and to compare it to what he left behind when he embarked on this journey. 'He came to himself' or, in other translations, 'he came to his senses' (Luke 15:17). Through reflection, he reaches some insight into his own life. Home appears in a different light now, and he considers going back. Conscious of what he has done, he is willing to settle for the lowest form of work on his father's farm, knowing that as a hired servant he can be dismissed at short notice. In his desperate situation, he finds enough freedom to begin the return journey, willing to beg for help. The life he embarked on has not worked out as he wanted or expected. Returning home, he is a different person now with a different disposition. Life has taught him some painful lessons.

As in the Emmaus story, the reverse journey begins with a different perspective and a different desire. In this case, however, there are limited expectations. The return of the Prodigal means, not just coming home to his family, but to some degree coming home to himself. He has no expectation of the reception he will receive. Willing to settle for the lowest grade, he is restored to full family membership, adorned with the rings, robes and sandals that only family members wear. The father's reaction – the watching, the running, the embracing, the lavish celebration – is more than a human response. The admission of human brokenness becomes an opening for the divine welcome. Coming from God's perspective, rather than a human one, the father's welcome and subsequent celebration open up an entirely new vision of life. The human situation is transformed by forgiving love.

This story has several stages:

- The younger son decides to leave the confinement of home for wider spaces.
- He asks for and gets his share of the inheritance.
- He goes far away to a distant land where he can live a life of self-indulgence, as he wants.
- In time, he runs out of resources and, influenced by the presence of famine, he has to make another decision.
- He hires himself out to do a demeaning job that would not have been acceptable back home.
- He begins to ponder his situation, coming to realise the predicament he has created for himself, and realising that the situation back home is not so bad after all.
- He decides to return home, seek forgiveness and beg for a menial job.
- He anticipates a difficult and painful reception on his arrival.
- To his amazement, he is greeted on his return by a great welcome and a lavish celebration.

All the decisions the Prodigal made thus far had a selfish dimension to them: his going away; his taking a job feeding pigs; and his coming back home. His concern is for himself. There are different hungers in him, though most attention is on the physical. It is implied, however, that a different hunger is also present, a hunger that is bringing him home in a new way, and of which he has little awareness. This hunger will need time to develop further before he can really realise what he has been truly lacking.

The Message of the Parable

We are left to take up the story from there ourselves. The life of self-gratification does not satisfy the Prodigal, leading to an inward, as well as an outward, search. His daydreams of happiness do not survive long once harsh reality hits him. External resources run out, and he is left alone to find his way. With his hopes for a new and better life dashed, his external situation causes him to reflect and to seek another way.

This is a story of freedom of different kinds. It is about going away and coming back, about what leads to 'death' and what leads to 'life'. We may indeed wonder how well the Prodigal knew the deeper reasons for his decisions, since there was a selfish dimension to all of them, including his decision to return home. The initial decision to leave home led to slavery, internal and external, while the second decision – to find a job feeding pigs, however distasteful – was a compromise to help him survive the crisis. The third decision, to return to his father, brought him home to himself and to his family. We may judge the Prodigal's first decision as foolish but, in a strange way, his going away enabled him to appreciate what awaited him on his return home. Having known slavery, he was better able to appreciate freedom and accept the gift offered to him. No doubt further decisions and adjustments would have to be made, as he grew in the realisation of what was offered to him.

Jesus used this parable as an illustration. It is a story of freedom and how it can be used poorly or well. It is a story of extravagant love and of family reconciliation. Above all, however, it is a story of the kind of God we have and what God desires for us. This is illustrated by the father, whose focus is entirely different from that of the son who has returned. The attention of the father is outward: he is focused on his son, as shown by the lavish and loving welcome he gives him on his return. The son's narrow world is shattered by the elaborate welcome and reception, but it will take some time for him to appreciate and accept that transforming love. He needs to find the freedom to be at home with that. Coming to reconciliation with himself may be a bigger challenge than coming to reconciliation with his father and his family.

Psychology can offer some understanding of what was going on for the Prodigal, including the different kinds of decisions involved. Freud, with his contribution to a more developed understanding of the unconscious and the power of the instinctual urges, can shed some light, at a human level, on the internal journey and the external behaviour of the Prodigal. Driven by his own immediate needs, according to this interpretation, reality set in for the Prodigal when his situation deteriorated, but all his decisions had a selfish element to them. John of the Cross and Ignatius would be able to identify with these selfish appetites and desires, but they would give a different reason for controlling them and redirecting the Prodigal's energy. John would see the son's appetites as blurring his vision and getting in the way of growth in the Lord. Ignatius, noting that the Prodigal was not at peace, would invite him to reflect on his life and to sift through his inner experiences, in order to see which ones were of God, which ones enhanced the Christ-quality of his life, and which ones gave enduring peace. Both John and Ignatius would direct the Prodigal away from selfish concerns into a freer way, rooted in the Lord. They would re-echo the teaching of Jesus in the parable that dissolute living does not bring the desired peace and happiness. We are made for more than that. Slavery to our immediate needs is not the way to true life.

The Prodigal's original ideal, with its longed-for freedom, seemed to have no limits, and it seemed that everything was possible. In due course – through the loss of resources, the scarcity of food, the poor conditions, and the lack of human support – reality made its presence felt and imposed limits. His life lacked the peace that would satisfy him in the longer term. He was surviving rather than living, and the situation pointed to deeper desires of which he had little awareness.

Our Journey Home
There are many influences at work in our lives and many layers to be peeled back if the truth that sets us free is to emerge. For a fuller understanding of the parable of the Prodigal, and of our own experience too, we have to go within to the underlying motivation, to the different influences that throw light on the decisions we make. This means getting in touch with the gift

within and how God is present in our life experience. Ignatius was familiar with daydreaming, but he learned to reflect on his daydreams and to see where they came from and where they led. He was guided by where he found enduring peace.

Jesus, knowing the history of his people as well as their everyday lives, spoke out of that knowledge. His parables were rooted in life, in nature, in people and in familiar work situations. Seeing the potential in his hearers to embrace his message, Jesus began at the human level, but through that he drew them into the deeper dimensions. That must be our way too if we wish to reach the kernel of his message. We need to take time for prayer and reflection to be raised beyond the everyday with its practical questions. The parable of the Prodigal is spoken in the context of Jesus' welcome for sinners and his friendship with them. In Luke 15, it is placed alongside the parables of the lost sheep and the lost coin, all of which end with finding and rejoicing. For us, that means finding God and finding our true selves.

The parable of the Prodigal can help us reflect on our faith journey, with its different invitations, and the dispositions required to respond to them. The story develops over time, as the son goes through different phases before deciding to return home. After his return the meaning of the entire experience will deepen for him with further reflection. As with all the parables, we have to write our own ending of the story, as it speaks to our own lives and our own situation. The story has not ended, but it brings us to a new phase that opens up further possibilities. In the parable, love and forgiveness are to become the way forward for the Prodigal and guide him on his onward journey. His focus on the past and its failures has been replaced by a future full of hope. The criteria for future decisions will be different. Change can happen.

We live in a world with all sorts of external influences, but the invitation is to begin with Christ, not ourselves. The Prodigal began with himself. He received gifts from his father, but those gifts were lost and he ended up with neither external possessions nor internal peace. The gifts he had received were used badly, but gifts were given to him once again on his return. Welcomed home in a loving way, his past no longer needed to be his focus, just as the past was never the father's focus. In the parable a shift takes place to the ideal that God offers: unconditional love in response to human failure.

We realise that, while the ideal world is without limits, in reality we live with limits. Theology and spirituality can present the ideal, but psychology helps explain why our responses are limited. Psychology helps us explore the struggle and the conflicts, explaining why there is mixed motivation and ambiguity, and why selfishness can take over. We can be selfish, but we also have great potential for generosity. The petty things of the everyday can catch us out, but challenge and crisis can enable us to forget ourselves and be readily available to others. This is implied in the story of the Prodigal. A different perspective and larger horizon inspire us to give without counting the cost. That horizon was opened up for the Prodigal on his return. God continues to offer a new horizon to us and to all who come to him.

The parable reminds us of the giftedness we possess as well as the frailty that we bear. It reminds us that we are creatures, however much we might like to be gods. It reminds us that we are human and limited, but that we possess great potential. Given the will, the freedom and the reason for doing so, this potential can be actualised, even though the environment and the circumstances of our lives can exercise contrary influences. A great deal depends on how we use the creative gifts given to us, and this requires self-knowledge, freedom and the motivation to be outward-looking. The Prodigal grew in self-knowledge through his experiences and his reflection, but this process didn't end with his homecoming. It would be ongoing for him.

Application of the Parable
The parable of the Prodigal Son is a very human story, set in a particular context, but with a deep and universal message. In it we see how God works through human weakness to present a beautiful message of love and reconciliation. It incarnates the love of Jesus who shares our humanity and who recognises our potential to grow in freedom and in love. In his search, the Prodigal made many mistakes but, on returning home, his experiences served to open a whole new horizon for him. He saw himself, his family and

his home in an entirely different way. The call now was to live out of that new perspective, to go deep within, to free his heart and to develop his potential for recognising God's presence in his story. Coming home did not mean going back to where he was before, but going forward in a new way, living out the love he had experienced.

The story of the Prodigal ends but does not end. Do you ever wonder what happened after the party? Doubtless the lives of all were changed. Relationships were different. The Prodigal's return brought about a new situation. The story provides direction for those of us who wish for liberation and service in the name of Jesus, bringing us to a point where we are invited to take up the story and write the next chapter. The story brings the son to a point of freedom that made the next step possible. Is that not what we do in spiritual direction? Its goal is to bring people to the point where Jesus, not the self, becomes the criterion for decisions. By inviting us to finish the story, Jesus is inviting us to come to the true meaning of what he desires for us: ongoing conversion, which reaches beyond the selfish to what is generous in the service of others.

The parable of the Prodigal facilitates self-knowledge, revealing to us the potential to choose well or poorly. It unveils to us a God of compassion who welcomes us in all situations. It helps us to deepen the reflective process that enhances our life in the Lord. It points to the gift that needs to be unwrapped, offers a message that sets hearts free, and opens the way to new life in the spirit of the resurrection. A great deal of what is central to spiritual direction can be found in this parable.

God offers his gift, but it needs an ongoing human response. God's way is the way of reconciliation – with God, self and others – as the source of true peace. It is our privilege to embrace this message, to give it flesh and blood in our own lives and to share it with others in spiritual direction. The human story, with its gifts and struggles, is the breeding ground for new life. The contribution of those who have helped us understand this story is invaluable, and gives us a solid base for our journey with and for the Lord. This journey is one that sets us free from internal and external slavery to become what we are created to be.

We continue onwards, knowing that the days of surprises have not ceased. Our generous God always has more gifts to share with us when we are ready to receive them. They are given so that we may share them with others in turn, to the glory of God. It is a privilege to be able to walk with others and share this great gift with them. In faith and love we continue this journey with and for the Lord, along with others who walk in his name, knowing that the Lord is always faithful.

Reflection

Where have I been most surprised by the Lord?
Has my understanding of spiritual direction changed in any way?
What is the invitation to me for the ongoing journey?

Appendix I: Cases for Discussion

Joe

Forty-year-old Joe has an MBA and works at executive level in a multinational IT company. He is married to Joan, who works as a legal secretary. They have two children, aged fourteen and eight. Joe, who has been with the company for more than ten years, has been promoted several times. Some of the other workers describe him as ambitious. His present position requires him to work extra hours, often at short notice, and it involves some foreign travel, which means considerable absence from the family. When he is at home he is tired much of the time, often falling asleep on the couch while watching sports on TV. He does not find much time to pray, and occasionally he sleeps late on Sunday and does not go to church, a new development for him. He blames it on his tiredness. Joan and the children are concerned about the quality of his presence to them, but Joe argues that he needs to hold on to a secure job in an uncertain economic climate. Besides, there are some more senior positions coming up in the next few years, and he does not want to jeopardise his chances of further promotion. He thinks that Joan and the children should try to understand his situation and be patient. He likes his work and feels he is doing a good job, as well as providing a good salary for his family which keeps them comfortable at a time when many of his contemporaries are less well off. He believes that if he gets the promotion he will have fewer demands for extra hours.

*What values, patterns and dynamics
do you note in Joe's life?*

Clare

Clare is forty-six and job-shares as a nurse. She has been married for twenty-one years to John, a teacher. They have three children, one of whom is at university, while the other two are in secondary school. Clare is described as caring and generous with her time, always willing to lend a hand. She likes being that way, reaching out to serve others, and she gets a lot of satisfaction from it. Her family think that she takes on too much, and feel that she can get frazzled at times. Martha, in Scripture, is an inspiration to Clare, since she was the one willing to help out (Luke 10:38–42). In fact, Clare thinks Martha was treated somewhat harshly in that scene – after all, if everyone sat around, nothing would get done. In prayer, she looks to the compassion of God, and identifies with Jesus reaching out to people, especially women like the Samaritan woman (John 4:1–30) and the widow at Nain (Luke 7:11–17). Clare belongs to a prayer group that meets regularly, but the leader of the group is moving and some of the members have asked Clare to replace her. Clare likes the group and finds it supportive. She feels there is no one else who can take on that role. Given her other commitments, her family is concerned about this. Having discussed it with them she has agreed to come and talk to you about her life, and about this decision, in particular.

What patterns do you notice in Clare's life?
How do they help you understand her?
Have you any comment to make on her prayer?
How would you help her?

Jimmy

Jimmy is thirty-five, a religious brother with a degree in French and English. While he did well in his degree, he is not very confident about teaching. He fears having exam classes, as he feels responsible for the pupils if they don't do well. For his first six years of teaching he worked in a smaller school in a rural town, where there was a friendly atmosphere and good support for him as a new teacher. Besides, he did not have any final-year exam classes. Recently he was moved to a major city, to teach in a school that has a reputation for success. He finds that there is rivalry between the teachers for success in exams. While his own classes have done OK in exams, there is constant pressure to keep up with the others. The environment is too competitive for his liking. He has talked to his superior about it, and was told to relax, that he was doing fine, and not to be so preoccupied with the other teachers. The superior added that it was good to have a brother in the school in the midst of the transition that was happening. Jimmy would like to move to a less stressful environment, but he feels under pressure to stay where he is. He finds it hard to pray, since he finds the demands of the Gospel and the cost of discipleship are so high. There is too much passion and not enough resurrection in the whole environment.

How do you understand Jimmy?
How would you help him?

Appendix II: The Conversion of Paul

Paul defends himself before King Agrippa
(Acts 26:1, 9–23)

Agrippa said to Paul, 'You have permission to speak for yourself'. Paul stretched out his hand and began to defend himself...

'I myself was convinced that I ought to do many things against the name of Jesus of Nazareth. And that is what I did in Jerusalem; with authority received from the chief priests, I not only locked up many of the saints in prison, but I also cast my vote against them when they were being condemned to death. By punishing them often in all the synagogues I tried to force them to blaspheme; and since I was so furiously enraged at them, I pursued them even to foreign cities. With this in mind, I was travelling to Damascus with the authority and commission of the chief priests, when at midday along the road, your Excellency, I saw a light from heaven, brighter than the sun, shining around me and my companions. When we had all fallen to the ground, I heard a voice saying to me in the Hebrew language, "Saul, Saul, why are you persecuting me? It hurts you to kick against the goads." I asked, "Who are you, Lord?" The Lord answered, "I am Jesus whom you are persecuting. But get up and stand on your feet; for I have appeared to you for this purpose, to appoint you to serve and testify to the things in which you have seen me and to those in which I will appear to you. I will rescue you from your people and from the Gentiles - to whom I am sending you to open their eyes so that they may turn from darkness to light and from the power of Satan to God, so that they may receive forgiveness of sins and a place among those who are sanctified by faith in me." After that, King Agrippa, I was not disobedient to the heavenly vision, but declared first to those in Damascus, then in Jerusalem and throughout the countryside of Judea, and also to the Gentiles, that they should repent and turn to God and do deeds consistent